LEAVING CANCER
FOR THE
CIRCUS

an american odyssey
inspired by love and recovery

BY
DANNY CLINKSCALE

FOREWORD BY KEVIN KIETZMAN

VENICE
COMMUNICATIONS, INC.

FIRST EDITION

ISBN-13: 978-1537368719
ISBN-10: 1537368710

Library of Congress Control Number: 2016914974

Editor: Mark Stallard

Cover Design: Lauren Goldman

All photographs courtesy of the author unless otherwise noted.

Venice Communications, Inc.
5503 Noland Road
Shawnee, Kansas 66216

CONTENTS

CONTENTS

LEAVING CANCER
FOR THE
CIRCUS

an american odyssey
inspired by love and recovery

*This book is dedicated with love to
my beautiful wife, Jayne.*

*Without her, there would be no trip and no book.
I trusted she would understand, and I was right.*

FOREWORD

BY

KEVIN KIETZMAN

Danny Clinkscale has done everything you can possibly do in sports radio, and there's a very good reason why — he can do anything. As you will undoubtedly discover in the pages of this book, when Danny sets his mind to something, he finishes it. It's the professional broadcaster and friend I want you to know first.

When Danny came to Sportsradio 810, we had a wide variety of new projects that needed attention, and we were hopeful Danny could help cover many of them. Truth is, they were things that nobody else wanted to do or could do. Like travel. You see, the most curious thing about my friend, who is so curious by nature, is that he loves hotels. From big, five star hotels in major metropolitan areas to tiny, little 24 room motels in small towns. I think he rates them based on their workout room. Soft, comfortable beds and marble bathroom counters are nice, but what kind of treadmills and elipticals do they have? He loves spending the night in Manhattan, Kansas, before hosting a Saturday morning College Gameday show in Aggieville at 9 a.m. A simpleton like me would roll out of bed, pour some caffeine, and hit the road. But Danny knows there is a workout room in a hotel somewhere with his name on it.

It all began when he started running like Forest Gump

every day, which was long before I knew Danny. His obsession to keep his 19-year, 5-month gotta-run every day streak alive reached critical mass one day in the Toronto airport. Danny somehow missed the Royals' charter flight home that was scheduled to land in time for him to run at the end of the day. The weather outside was horrible. Danny's bags were on the plane. So Danny buys a pair of running shoes at the airport and proceeds to start running all-around the concourses. I'm not talking about some 15-minute jog here; Danny ran for 4 miles just inside the fence on the tarmac ... I would give anything to have video of him running that day.

He plays golf religiously and will gladly play by himself. Danny is the only guy I've ever met who will golf in shorts when it's 38 degrees, and he'll play even when there's nobody working at the clubhouse that day. The point is, Danny attacks things and doesn't let go.

Like beating cancer.

Danny was so good at beating cancer that he never complained, barely missed work and to my knowledge never, ever once asked, "Why me?" After his initial surgery, when they found it to be worse than doctors thought, I'm pretty sure there was a little scare. But Danny quickly came back to work and moved forward. He would leave the office a lot for treatment and for the most part, only me and Todd Leabo knew when Danny was coming and going. We told him to take it easy at work, don't sweat it, and to focus on beating this thing. But Danny didn't really want others to know what was going on. Well into his treatments one day, Danny was out of the office and somebody asked me if Danny was around. I just quickly reacted by saying, "he's getting radiation treatment today, probably back tomorrow."

The co-worker responded that he had completely forgotten Danny had cancer and please don't mention it. What they didn't know is Danny would take that as a compliment. He wanted everyone to forget about it and just go about business as usual.

And for Danny, business is good.

I mentioned earlier Danny can do anything and it's really quite amazing. He can literally go from discussing European Soccer to NASCAR without any notes or preparation if he needs to. Danny's been on the show with me for so long I don't remember the shows before he joined us. But it's all the other projects he attacks that leave his co-workers in wonder. He quickly started hosting College Gameday, one of the most successful sports shows in Kansas City radio history. Danny has done play-by-play for UMKC, the Kansas City T-Bones, high school football, MLS Soccer, and golf just at WHB. He has covered pretty much every major sporting event in America and as you will read, has a particular fondness of the 2014 MLB post season. Danny was on the road, and, on the road to recovery. The Royals were suddenly good. That's when Danny Clinkscale proved to all of us once again that when he starts something, he finishes it.

Kevin Kietzman
August 2016

Now in his 20th year hosting Between the Lines *on Sportsradio 810 WHB, Kevin Kietzman is recognized by* Sports Illustrated, Radio Ink, Talkers Magazine, *and Sportsradio.com as one of the top Sports Talk Show Hosts in America. A Kansas City native, he grew up in Mission, Kansas, attended Kansas State University, and began his broadcasting career on the K-State student radio station his freshman year. Kietzman has done radio and television play-by-play, worked as a sports reporter and anchor at KOAM-TV in Pittsburg, KS/Joplin, MO, and served 10 years as a sports reporter and anchor at WDAF-TV Fox 4 in Kansas City.*

Prologue

AGE 0
SOCIABLY LATE

I was born in Brattleboro, Vermont on August 6. Throughout my life I have always tried to be a nice person, and I guess that started even before I was born. I was pretty obviously a honeymoon night baby. However, the actual gestation period for a human being is not a full nine months, it is several days shy of that. So when my mother was informed that her first child was due on July 28, she was horrified.

I took matters into my unborn hands by arriving one week late—*nine months to the day*—after my parents were married, thus saving my mom's deserved good reputation.

I have never been back to Brattleboro, and don't know much about it except that it isn't supposed to be much of a spot, an industrial town gone to seed. At a recent Final Four I was covering for 810 WHB, and approached Tom Brennan,

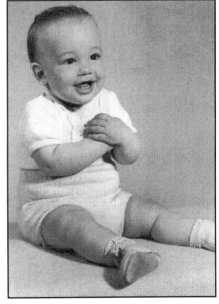

Baby Clinkscale, ready for all the world has to offer.

1

the former longtime coach at the University of Vermont, and asked him if he had ever recruited anyone from Brattleboro. I explained that's where l was born, and asked if it was worth going there sometime.

"Oh, God no, don't bother going there," he quickly shot back. "You don't want to go there."

Alrighty then.

1.

VANISHING INTO THE SAND

It was October 27, 2014. I sat in my car in the parking lot at the Kansas City International airport after flying back from San Francisco, where I had covered games 3, 4, and 5 of the World Series. The night before, the Giants, behind the all-world excellence of pitcher Madison Bumgarner, had won game 5 to take a three games to two lead over the Kansas City Royals.

So, I was sitting in the car and I did what you might do a few times a day—I scratched a little itch on the left side of my face. But this time I felt something under the surface of the skin, a small lump. In other circumstances I wouldn't have thought anything of it. I had led a remarkably healthy life, and I seldom thought about health issues. If there was a little something wrong, I generally ignored it and let it pass.

About a year earlier, I had outpatient skin cancer surgery for a small issue on my left temple, so this time I was far more proactive than I ever would have been otherwise. The discovery of the lump ignited the process that would ultimately lead to my own American Odyssey.

• • • • •

It was a big thrill for someone whose favorite sport is baseball to get to be the main post-season correspondent for Sportsradio 810 WHB—Kansas City's top sports station—and the sole person who traveled. I had the same opportunity in the American League Championship Series when the Royals swept the Orioles. That meant two games in Baltimore at Camden Yards, one of baseball's most enjoyable venues. Same for AT&T Park in San Francisco, and the same back in Kansas City as the Royals' electrified fans turned Kauffman Stadium into a wonderful, wild carnival.

The thing is, it's a little less glamorous than you might imagine at these gigantic events now. Unless you are a major city columnist, or work for ESPN or FOX, there is not enough actual press box space. So the media game seats are often in the outer reaches of the ball park. No complaints, this is the pinnacle of the game, and we have a great setup with televisions and assistance. But many of the fans have far better seats compared to ours.

So, in the midst of one of the more enjoyable, busiest, and gratifying assignments of my career, the health process began. In this case, I had the lump checked out fairly quickly. Long story short, it turned out to be a combination of a health issue and bad luck. It was likely that a small piece of the previous skin cancer had broken loose and unfortunately penetrated my main salivary gland. This was considered somewhat fluky, but that matters little.

I guess I'm not a very good listener when it comes to these things, because it never registered to me that it was malignant. My thought was that they would do the operation, and then find out if it was malignant or not. This did not make for a very happy wife when I came out of about six hours of surgery in January 2015, and she had been told what the reality actually was. I truly did not know, and was not trying to hide anything from anyone.

The surgery was brilliantly done. Within a few months the scarring would be almost unrecognizable. But of course there were quite a few things to deal with. I had to undergo 30 treatments of radiation, although I did not have to go through chemotherapy. This meant zapping me right by my voice box, which is my livelihood. Also, for a while as the healing took place, my neck was pretty ugly. I wore high-necked clothes and ruined quite a few shirts, but there was not a considerable amount of discomfort. It was no day at the beach either.

The radiation process was not that onerous. Starting in mid-February I did the treatments daily each weekday. They were scheduled for 10 a.m. each day, and it only took 30-45 minutes per day due to the varying waiting times. The treatments themselves only took about 15 minutes. I wore a giant fitted mesh mask, laid down flat, and was zapped with lasers.

The nurses at KU Medical Center were wonderful. I wore a necklace that had to be taken on and off each day, and they kind of made it a game as to who would do that chore. I will say that I will never watch "The Price is Right" ever again, even if I ever wanted to. It was on the television in the waiting room each day as I waited for treatment. I saw the same faces in the waiting room each day. I was envious of the people ending their treatment and empathetic of those just beginning as my time was winding down.

I developed a relationship with an older gentleman who was about on the same timetable as me. He had a bit of a European accent I couldn't quite identify. We never exchanged names or anything, just started out acknowledging each other daily, and eventually having short conversations. My last day I gave him my card, and we exchanged a couple of embraces.

It was pretty emotional. Just two strangers sharing something important, but fleeting.

The side effects were not awful, but not insignificant either. I slowly lost all of my ability to taste. If it was just no taste that wouldn't have been so bad, but things actually tasted bad. At the worst, my analogy was that everything tasted as if I were chewing a piece of gum with the silver wrapper still on it. My mouth constantly tasted as if I had been swimming in the ocean all day. There was slow improvement over time, but I did lose a fairly considerable amount of weight, about 25 pounds and I probably only needed to lose about 10.

I worked out every day, and I worked every day. When it was suggested that maybe I should take a little time off, my thought was why should I waste time off when I felt just a little crummy. It was at this time, about March 1, that I started to hatch my plan of taking off, just getting away by myself to some areas of the upper Midwest and a little west of that, which I had never really explored.

Right from the outset, I felt like my little getaway had to be somewhat of a secret, something that would be just for me to own, and think about, at times when I needed a goal. There was, however, nothing devious in my mind about it. I would have to tell a couple of people at work for planning reasons, and I shared it with my youngest sister, who I am very close with despite the fact that we live far apart, and we actually don't communicate constantly. Besides that, I just kept it close to my heart.

I guess this is a good time to explain the logic (or lack thereof) of not discussing this with the most important person in my life, my wife, Jayne. The guys who knew about this thought I was insane, which was probably a bit true. But to me it's the

My Note to My Wife

Darling,

This is a love letter.

I will grant that it is an unconventional one, but I see it that way. The fact that I love you so much, and trust you, and have great faith in our relationship, and believe that the feeling is completely mutual, has allowed me to feel good about the flight of fancy I am about to embark on. It was hatched mentally almost three months ago during some of the most challenging days of radiation.

I am going on a guy trip, with one significant difference to most. There's one guy. Me. When you read this, you will be the last person I know who I will have any significant contact with. I will be driving north. I know where I am stopping tonight. That is all I know. I have no real plan. Around March 1, I made a map of the northern midwest. I would look at it when I was in the waiting room, or in my cubby hole at work. It was something that gave me something to look ahead to. I wasn't, and am not now, sad or mad, just wistful. I think I did a pretty good job of muscling through the process, but this idea gave me a boost when I needed it. I have some ideas of little towns, or scenic areas, etc. that seem interesting, but I am going to take it as it comes.

I will have my phone off most of the time, but I will check it for emergencies. I will make sure you know daily by text that I am safe, and where I am, and no doubt how much I love you. I imagine solitude will only increase that feeling. I plan on perhaps occasionally posting Americana photos on Facebook with no comment except location. I will have my computer, but view it sparingly. I will only be gone about ten days.

Only three people really know much of anything about this. Obviously, a few other people know I am going to be on vacation, that was mandatory. But only Kevin and Todd, for obvious reasons, and my sister Colleen really know. Colleen and I talked about this long ago when I was just kind of pondering it. I wanted one other person who would be able to talk to you, that you could trust, who would assure you that this was not some kind of midlife crisis, or in any way was a reflection of any dissatisfaction of my home life. Pure and simple it was a goal to have when I felt I needed one. She didn't think it was nuts, so I guess that's something, or maybe she is, too. The fact that I wanted to speak with nobody about it, including the person I care about the most, was just a reflection of the fact this was something that would be mine, start to finish. The trip ends up being far more about the thought of it than what ends up happening as I depart.

I never thought this might be the case, but if you think this whole thing is the worst idea in the world, please forgive me. If you understand, thank you. I believe this will be an enriching experience for me. I will not be melodramatic, I don't *need* to do this, but I believe it will be helpful, and a way to move forward. I look forward very much to returning to my very good life, and the normalcy of my day to day life. I look forward to our anniversary, and I look forward to the next, more exotic, vacation with you. You are the best traveling companion one can imagine, and the best life companion.

I love you more and more.

Danny

ultimate testimony as to how strong the relationship with my wife is. I was about 96 percent sure she would have no issue with the trip, and would truly understand the reasons for it. If there was the slightest of chances in my mind she wouldn't like it, I was going to go anyway, so this was my way of ensuring that my getaway would take place.

But mostly, I just wanted to own it. To know each day leading up to the late May departure, what I was going to do, and no one else would. My sister was a bit of a conduit as well. While I would write a heartfelt email upon departure to my wife, I needed someone that Jayne could trust to tell her that this was a long planned and personal odyssey that had nothing to do with any trivial, or important, matters in our life. It was merely about my navigation away from a stressful issue in my own way.

This was all important because a big part of the whole deal in my mind was that there would be no communication with the regular parts of my world. I wanted that to be part of the whole process. I would text my wife each evening, stating only my whereabouts and that I was safe and sound. As some of my Facebook friends know, I would post some pictures, but without comment, only noting the location.

I made myself a rather shabby map of the region, which I would have out in my work area in the months leading up to the scheduled departure. I never actually made a solid plan, but I did spend hours thinking about possible routes, and stops, and potential things to do. But most of what I would do was ... nothing. Lots of driving and gazing at a beautiful part of our country. I also decided early on that the driving would preclude interstate highways, and I was pretty much able to stick with that plan.

There had long been in place a remote radio broadcast at Firekeeper Golf Course in Mayetta, Kansas, for the end of May. That became the planned time for my journey to begin. As the months turned to weeks, and the weeks turned to days for my time to set out on the road, things certainly became exciting. Everything was starting to really work as I planned. When my food didn't taste so good, or I felt like I had to sleep a little more, or all the water I was consuming was resulting in extra bathroom visits at night, I knew that I would soon only have to answer to myself on the road.

Among many things that were most appealing was to not have any responsibilities in any given day. I could get up when I wanted, drive when I wanted, stop when I wanted, eat when I wanted (although not enough progress had been made for that to be much of an issue), and choose what I would do without any restrictions. I never slept until noon. I never went to bed at eight. I didn't really try anything exotic. The things I always like to do would fill my days, but they would be at my leisure, and of my choosing.

In daydreams of the past, I had often thought if I had no responsibilities, and had reasonably unlimited resources, and maybe wasn't lucky enough at that time to have loved ones close at hand, that I would like to tour the country, or continent for that matter. Perhaps get a Winnebago, and for months, just go.

This getaway is my miniature version of that. There will be plenty of time to think, and along the way, in my reminiscing, I will drop in some small chapters of years from my life that were particularly significant and led me to this place in my life, a place that is very good—I have a wonderful wife, great kids,

As I started my odyssey, the lonely highways held nothing but promise for my one-man adventure.

a job I love working with extraordinary people, and a whole lot more. But for just a little while, I will leave that behind.

Here I go.

2.

THE NUT ON THE ROOF

May 29, 2015 - Day 1
Mayetta, Kansas to Broken Bow, Nebraska - 325 miles

So, my American odyssey begins. As the day dawns, this is the only morning that I actually will know my eventual destination. I wanted to put a stake in the ground and commit to actually starting this trip around the middle of April. It just so happened that I had a remote broadcast at Firekeeper Golf Course and Prairie Band Casino out of town in Mayetta, Kansas, in late May. Here was my chance, so I decided this was the moment I should just go.

I figured on the first day I'd like to make a good chunk of time and distance. As I said, I also am committed to not driving on any interstates if at all possible. So I get out my trusty make-shift map that I made and looked about 350 miles northwest, and I settled on Broken Bow, Nebraska. The historic Arrow Hotel will be the luxury high point of lodging on this escapade. It was inexpensive for the quality, but I was looking to start on a high note. With my bike along, and no gym required, I will be looking for pure value if I don't sleep in a campground.

The unofficial (if anything is official here) start of the trip was the two days at Prairie Band. The "Stay and Play" that we promote with remote broadcasts on Sportsradio 810 is great fun. Play a little golf, stay at the casino, and promote a very promotable product. I do it annually, and it is very enjoyable. The people there are great, as you will hear again later.

I started off after the Mayetta days in rainy weather. The 350 miles would include 64 degrees and rainy, 80 degrees and sunny, back to spitting rain, temperature dropping to 55 degrees with brisk wind as the destination drew closer. Typical Midwest. Switching from flatlands to rolling terrain, partially through the Flint Hills, it is heartland driving and scenery that seems for the moment at its best, with better to come I am sure. Vast fields of rolling greenery, restful cattle lying about or eating, and birds with all the sky in the world to fly about in.

Of course, then there are the delights of the radio. I have worked in it my whole life, so I am clearly biased, but I love the companionship. I can do silence with the best of them for good stretches, but you combine music, old-time dramas, baseball, and of course some sports talk and you've got something.

Today's fare included the Royals' win over the Cubs (Chicago broadcast), The Mavericks' latest CD "Mono," two episodes of "The Saint" with Vincent Price, "Have Gun Will Travel," and WHB, which lasted well into the middle of Nebraska. I'm giving my favorite Mark Knopfler music a couple of days breather.

• • • • •

Baseball on the radio is one of my life's greatest pleasures. I am of a generation weaned far more on listening than on watching baseball. I have broadcast thousands of baseball games, and while from a creative and kinetic standpoint, I like doing play-by-play of basketball the most, for listening, a baseball game can't be beat.

I have hundreds of interesting listening stories, and about as many broadcasting ones. For right now, we'll keep it to one of each. During the 1979 baseball season, my beloved, but often downtrodden Houston Astros appeared poised to win something for the very first time. I became an Astros fan based on the exploits of César Cedeño, whose play in the 1970s at an extremely young age, rightfully drew comparisons to Willie Mays.

Cedeño had already started a slight decline as a player, but he gifted (or cursed) me with lifelong Astros fanhood. In 1979, the Astros had exploded to a 10-game lead in the National League West by the All-Star break time. My girlfriend at the time had even made me a hideous, but thoughtful, "Houston Astros 1979 NL West Champions" T-shirt. I was appalled at the surefire curse of that, but she had no idea about such things. It was a nice gesture.

Predictably, the pedigree of the Cincinnati Reds started to take over, and the lead dwindled. Late in the summer, just before returning to the University of Kansas, the Reds and Astros had a key series in Cincinnati. Here I am living at my parents' house in Framingham, Massachusetts, and on an August night, I sat on the roof of the house, in the rain, with an umbrella, and my radio tuned to WLW in Cincinnati. That's what I get for abandoning my hometown Red Sox, whom I rooted for until age 12.

WLW was a 50,000 watt clear-channel AM station and at night, sometimes intermittently, you *could* hear Marty Brennaman, the voice of the Reds, call the game. An occasional car on the dead end street would go by and slow down to look at the nut on the roof of the house on Brookvale Road.

The Astros would lose the division in 1979 by a game and a half, but triumphantly take the division the following year, only to lose a sickeningly tight NLCS to the Phillies in a decisive fifth game. The Phillies of course, would go on to beat the Royals in the World Series.

One of many bizarre and wonderful play-by-play tales comes in the late 1980s when I was broadcasting games in the New York-Penn league for the Utica Blue Sox. It was, and is, a short season single A league, mostly players just drafted in the June draft. One of the opponents in the league was the Auburn Astros. Auburn now has a wonderful minor league park, pretty much a necessity if you are going to keep a team.

Back then, many teams, including Utica, and in this case Auburn, played in old fairgrounds-style parks. Among the issues when you did a game in Auburn was the drive, the longest in the league for games we broadcast. That was made worse by the fact I was also doing the morning drive then, and had to be at work at the radio station at 4 a.m. But the biggest issue was the fact that they had built the diamond in Auburn the wrong way, meaning that in the heart of the summer, the sun set over the center field fence.

Not only did that mean it was about 185 degrees in the wooden press box, but worst of all, on a sunny day, for player safety, there was a "sun delay." About the third inning the sun would be low in the sky and in the batters' eyes, so we would have to stop for 30-45 minutes. Which meant yours truly, doing the game alone, would get to fill all that air time. There was never a happier man when it was a cloudy evening in Auburn, New York.

Mankato, Kansas. I didn't spend much time in this little town.

• • • • •

You see lots of interesting things when you drive. Most communities tout their downtowns as "historic," even if they now feature empty storefronts, but a few actually are worthy of the historic tag. A town can't make up being the geographical center of the United States, which is where Lebanon, Kansas, lies. If you stop and take a picture (which I did), you can't really *feel* that you are in the center of anything, but darn it, it's true.

The very first gas stop on my sojourn was Mankato, Kansas. Actually, I have heard of Mankato, Minnesota. That's where the Kansas City Chiefs used to go scrimmage the Vikings when Minnesota trained there, and the Chiefs trained in River Falls, Wisconsin. After a couple of years of regular fights, the two teams stopped that little arrangement. I do miss the time when the Chiefs trained in River Falls.

The Chiefs now train in St. Joseph, Missouri, and it is probably the right thing. The fans can get there easily, and the Missouri taxpayers, who paid millions for stadium improvements, probably deserve the convenience of seeing their heroes without a major trip.

But there was something kind of cool about going to the tiny Division III university town for camp. First off for the fans, they actually had to make a somewhat major commitment to support their favorite team. I wouldn't burn my summer vacation on watching football practice, but many families, especially at the height of Chiefs mania, did just that. There were lots of outdoor activities like hunting and fishing, you could skip over to the Mall of America, or perhaps catch a Twins' game at the Metrodome, since Minneapolis was only about an hour away.

For the media, there was sort of an "off to camp" feeling. You worked long hours, and then there were only a handful of places to go in River Falls, so just about everybody would gather at the same places. That might spill out to Hudson or Stillwater, both on the Mississippi River in Minnesota. They were very cool little downtowns, with nice places on the water. There was a neat bit of camaraderie among the media on these visits. But those days are gone and the Mankato of the present, in Kansas, is the first way station of my journey.

Mankato, Kansas, is a *very* little town. You see things in 2015 in small places that still are surprising. I went into the gas station on US 36. The pump was just that, a gas pump, no way to pay at the pump. OK, I went inside and grabbed a couple of items and went to the counter. A very nice young lady was working, I put the items on the counter, she rang them up and I told her I wanted $30 on pump 2. She very nicely told me that

I had to go out and pump the gas first. There was no automatic shut-off function. I pumped the gas and went back in and settled up. As I left she smiled and said, "You see things in a little town like this you don't often see anymore."

Yes, you do.

• • • • •

So I was officially off and running. The first night's stop as mentioned is Broken Bow, Nebraska. It was selected purely for the distance from Mayetta, and for the fact that it seemed to fit the kind of place that I wanted to spend most nights. A small town, but with reasonable lodging. The Arrow Hotel would turn out to be high-cotton luxury accommodations compared to what would follow. It was an old, refurbished hotel and I had a suite. It was basically a little apartment with three rooms, including a full kitchen. That's two rooms more than I planned on having for the rest of the trip. It was a nice way to get things started.

Of course this thing wouldn't have happened at all without the support of my wife and my great co-workers at WHB, even if only a couple of them knew what I was going to set out on. Kevin Kietzman and Todd Leabo are the people I work the closest with each day on the great staff, and they were among the few co-conspirators.

They are truly superb people to work with and for, and they were so understanding during the time when I was kind of just grinding through the days. They had their doubts about some of the details of my little plan, but had often prodded me to take some time. As I mentioned before, I wanted to wait to enjoy the time more.

The end of each day's drive on most of my journey was kind

I received a great small-town welcome in Broken Bow, Nebraska, to get me started on the odyssey.

of the same. I would pull into town, a little worn-out from the driving, and would generally do something to get a little energy. I might take a quick run, or a bike ride, or a nap. On this first night, I just took a shower and watched a little TV, and then drove a bit around the town to see if there was a place that might be fun on a Friday night. It became clear that the bar and restaurant at the Arrow Hotel was the place in town to gather.

It was called The Bonfire and was no wild hot spot, but it was lively, and at the very least provided an opportunity for one of my favorite sports ... people watching. There was a very busy waitress working the tables at the restaurant/bar, and she fit into a certain mold. A once lovely young lady who still was in good shape, but had clearly smoked about a million cigarettes. She looked like she was about 50, but she might have not yet quite cracked 40.

I have always found that a little sad, and it has always made me glad that I never started smoking cigarettes. I think I gave one a try when I was about 10, and once again around age 21. So that's the total for me ... two cigarettes.

The younger girl who was working the bar had some bad news for me. I was one week too early for "Big Kahuna Night." There were a host of posters around touting the incredible fun that was to be had on this festive occasion. But alas, it was seven days hence. As it turned out, on my way back, there was only one small stretch where I retraced some steps, and on the next Friday I went back through Broken Bow. Perhaps not shockingly, I had forgotten that it was going to be "Big Kahuna Night" that very evening. I didn't stop. Did I do the right thing? The excitement potentially missed probably is better just in the imagination.

There was never any trouble sleeping on this trip. Most days included a whole lot of things, plus a healthy dose of driving. I don't think I cracked midnight except once. You'll have to wait for that, and there is hardly much bacchanalia to be reported.

As I closed my eyes, I smiled. Life has always been pretty darn good to me, and the one major thing that wasn't right now was starting to recede. I had several more days to explore and feel the sensations and see the sights. I also would have a lot of time to think about the path that I had taken to this journey. I was doing a little processing of that as the day came to an end and I slipped into my dreams.

3.

COMFORTABLE INTRUDER

May 30, 2015 - Day 2
Broken Bow, Nebraska to Hot Springs, South Dakota -
305 miles

One of the real joys (among a million) of this trip as I move forward will be having my bicycle along. The first reason for it is simple economics. Because I can't run daily anymore, but I do work out every day, I usually want at least a decent gym. Well, that requires a reasonably good hotel, and considering where I want to go, and the fact that I want to not spend thousands, I want to be able to stop ... wherever.

These days that means bicycling. Which is very cool anyway, since when I go to these smallish towns and cities, every morning, and sometimes also in the evening when I arrive, I can pretty much cover the entire town in one ride.

Now once upon a time the solution would have been even simpler, when I was a daily runner. I could probably write a book about my 19-year and five-month, 7,131 consecutive day running streak. In fact, I know I could. It started with no real goal when I was 29 and ended just shy of my 50th birthday.

• • • • •

I will only give a couple of stories regarding it, otherwise, the streak *would* be another book. I began running avidly in my mid-20s, and a few years later I ran in my first road race, a 10K that was shorter than the distance I ran every day. My regular running route at the time was just over 7 miles, and a 10K is just over six. When I did my regular route I never drank water on the way. In fact, in addition to the seven-mile daily runs, on Sundays I usually ran 12-14 miles. So I didn't think a 10K was any particular challenge.

But the day was much warmer than expected. I ran my daily runs fairly fast, usually around seven minute miles. This was my first race, I was no doubt a little fired up, so I was running faster than that. I literally was stupidly scoffing at the thought of using the water stations. It would take it's toll. My younger brother Jim was riding a bike along the route encouraging me. With about a mile to go, he told me I was in ninth place and that eighth was about 100 yards ahead, and he encouraged me to catch him. I replied, "Jim, I ain't catching anybody." I was exhausted.

I literally don't remember the final mile. There was a group of friends and family waiting at the finish line. My brother had ridden ahead and told them I was in ninth. They watched as the eighth place, ninth place, 10th place runners finished. No sign of me. Then my sister-in-law looked in the other direction, and about 50 yards away I was laying in the street. I had blindly turned the wrong way at the end.

I had heat exhaustion and severe dehydration. I was rushed to the hospital and my temperature registered higher than the thermometer which topped at 108 degrees. The doctors told me later if the hospital had been any further away than the 3 miles that it was, I would have died. I was out for about eight hours, but I made it through.

I had been running daily then for a couple of years, The doctor told me not to run for a month ... so I skipped one day. That day was the last one I would miss for almost 20 years. Eventually the rule of thumb for me was that it had to be at least 4 miles, and it had to be outside. Of course that wasn't much of a bar early on, but as time went on, time constraints sometimes got in the way of a longer run, so I made the little rule. I ran in the rain, deep snow, 100-degree heat, with broken ribs, with a separated shoulder, and so on, but the biggest challenge one day was sports and work related, so I will tell that story.

The first year that I worked at WHB was 2000, and the first baseball season was 2001. I had done all kinds of baseball coverage when I worked previously at KMBZ, which held the Kansas City Royals' rights. The Royals had a (you may be surprised at this) promising year in 2000, with a powerhouse offense. Three Royals drove in 100 runs, three also scored 100 runs. The feeling was with a little added pitching, they might actually contend.

So the plan was for me to be the road correspondent for the radio station. Boy, do I wish that the Royals had fulfilled that hope, since I did the first three road trips, and it was one sweet assignment. I like to travel, I like big cities and hotels, and I love baseball.

Unfortunately, the Royals tanked right out of the box, and the day that challenged the streak would be the last one I covered on the road before we pulled the plug on our road game coverage. The Royals had already been in Toronto, but they had a game postponed due to roof problems at what was then the Skydome.

So after playing games in Tampa and Boston, they had a one-off makeup date in Toronto. When we finished up in Boston, they asked that we send some luggage ahead. Seeing as it was an afternoon game and our flight plans would have us back in KC about 8 o'clock, I just figured I would run then.

When the Royals played a getaway day, I would go to the clubhouse, gather some sound, check the board where the bus time for departure to the airport was listed, and then head to my broadcast location. I was traveling on the charter, and obviously on their schedule. I would tell the guys back at the station how long the postgame segment would be, and pack up to arrive about five minutes early or so for departure.

While I was upstairs doing my segment, the Royals received a call from the airport telling them that if they could arrive early, they had a takeoff window that would save considerable time. Knowing nothing about this, and also not realizing they didn't care too much about the tagalong radio reporter who was not on either of their network broadcasts, I arrived in the bowels of Skydome at 4:38, seven minutes ahead of the listed 4:45 departure.

There was no sign of anyone. I frantically asked around and everyone was pretty clueless. Finally, a clubhouse attendant told me that they had left early, and I was stranded in Toronto. This was no real emergency as far as regular life was concerned, and frankly, not an emergency as far as my now 15-year running streak was concerned ... yet.

I figured that I would just stay the night in Toronto, find a store and buy some cheap running clothes and shoes, and get a nice evening run in and everything would be cool. But when I called back to Kansas City, I was told that due to some staffing issues the next day, they wanted me to take the last flight out of Toronto on this day, so I could work a full day on Tuesday.

For most people that would be no big deal, but when I heard the itinerary, I was panicking. It was now 5:30 ... the flight was at 8:45 ... there was a layover ... and arrival in Kansas City was 12:40 a.m. That would mean that Monday, April 30, would include no run. I was not going to let this stand in my way if I could pull it off.

I flagged down a cab, told him I needed to go to a Payless Shoe Source. I dashed in and bought a pair of low-grade running shoes. There was a cheapo store right next to the Payless that had basic athletic wear, so I now had that covered. But I needed help. This was pre-9/11, so there was a chance I could still keep the streak alive.

I went to the gate. It was 7:30 now. Of course if it were today, there would have been significant security *and* you wouldn't be able to go in and out easily. I spoke to the lady at the gate, and gave her my tale, telling her how much it would hurt to watch my 15-year streak go down the tubes due to bad logistics. She agreed to help, I went to the restroom, took off my dress clothes, threw on the running stuff, and went back to the gate and gave her the clothes.

At 7:45 I was out on the airport grounds, and ran about 4 miles in a half-hour. Back in, back to the desk, got my clothes, splashed myself a tad bit clean, and got to the gate at 8:30. The streak was rescued, thanks to desperate industry from me, and the understanding of an airline employee.

I almost always ran first thing in the day, but not all the time, if it was inconvenient for whatever reason. From that day forward, I vowed to do it first thing no matter what. That meant some 3:30 a.m. runs in sub-freezing temperatures, but I knew that it was out of the way, and no circumstance could change that.

Well, until my knee exploded five years later. I was doing some light basketball practice for a charity event that WHB was going to do. My co-worker Soren Petro was there. I was merely doing layups when I went up to shoot, and the next thing I know I was flat on my back, and Soren was screaming at me not to look down at my leg. Of course I did, and got to see that my kneecap was about a foot from where it should be, in my upper thigh.

By the time the paramedics came, the kneecap had on its own somewhat returned closer to its natural location. They wrapped it up, and I started naively thinking that maybe I could tough it out the next day and keep the streak alive. At the hospital, the doctor took one look at it, and asked me to lift my leg. I couldn't raise it an inch. He told me they would do the X-Rays, but he pretty much knew it was a ruptured patellar tendon. Which it was.

It's probably the worst knee injury you can get, and after all the rehab, I still go running some, but not lengthy streaks. If I happened to be staying in a place with no easy gym access I would do it, or if I was staying in a major city. I love city running. But if I do it five, six days in a row I really start to feel it. We have an elliptical in the basement and some weights, and that's what I do.

As time has gone by, I even run less. Unfortunately, it is just better for the wear and tear to use other methods of exercise.

So my trusty mountain bike would join my golf clubs as two of the few things that would be close friends for the trip.

. . . . .

The first small town ride came this morning in Broken Bow. As I mentioned, the great thing about it, is that in a 60-75 minute ride you could generally cover all or most of one of these communities.

It's a nice town, the county seat of Custer County and just about smack dab in the middle of Nebraska. On a beautiful morning I roll past the county courthouse, and the softball fields next to a nice town park, and the fairgrounds (I'll be seeing a bunch of those), and on into some residential neighborhoods.

I very much enjoyed, when I ran, and enjoy now on my bicycle, going through neighborhoods and letting my mind wander toward some speculation about what is going on in the homes and little businesses wherever I go. I've never worn headphones or anything like that when I exercise outside. It's just me and my wandering mind.

In Broken Bow, I saw the first example on this trip of a rather common recurring theme. When you are in older neighborhoods in smaller communities, there is often a jarring juxtaposition of the care and pride taken in homes. Here most of the houses were very tidy middle class homes. But then one would pop up, a very ill-cared for place with a bad lawn that hadn't been tended to at all. With a home with a paint job very badly needed.

It can't be considered very neighborly, and I often muse about what it is that has these people in a position where they don't care at all, or have any pride in where they reside. I'm sure that conversation takes place very often in the kitchens of the tidy houses next door.

After a great ride, I had a nice shower in my little mini-apartment of sorts at the Arrow Hotel, which I kind of savored because I knew that the accommodations were going to get a bit more spartan soon enough. On the road with 315 miles under my belt yesterday, I plotted out about 300 miles for the next stop, toward the Northwest.

I picked out Hot Springs, South Dakota, for today's destination. I wanted to do lots of miles the first few days, and then maybe take it a little easier whenever I decided to head back. Taking Route 2 out of Broken Bow, I had a gorgeous day to drive. I would quickly be getting into the Sand Hills, and what would be a slowly escalating level of beautiful views.

As I settled in for the drive, a feeling of real happiness was evident. I had a real sense of why I had decided to do this, and now with everyone aware of it, and showing approval and support, I really just felt great. And excited. And emotional. I have always been a reasonably emotional person, although most people around me don't necessarily see that. But this experience, and the support I have had ... all of it kind of hit me.

There is little doubt that going through surgery and treatment has escalated that emotion. Scenes in a movie, or a great song, or just thinking about my wife, or my kids, can make me start to mist up kind of easily. I am completely comfortable with it, although sometimes I even surprise myself when it occurs.

Late lunchtime would come in Mullen, Nebraska, a very tiny community known to me before only because Sand Hills Golf

A beautiful view, just outside of Hot Springs, South Dakota.

Club is outside of this town. It is a famous 36 hole destination that you have to work very hard to get to, or have your own private plane. It will be a later part of this story.

I stopped just off Route 2 in Mullen at a little roadside diner, after I pumped gas across the street at a place where even in the middle of the day, all you could get is gas. There wasn't a soul there, just put the credit card in the pump. Then I went across the dusty road for lunch. And I was now on Mountain time.

When I stepped inside, there was a small gathering of folks, and I think folks is just the right word, because they were all by my guess, farmers or retired farmers. Cowboy hats on most heads. My hair still isn't growing in the back, so there was no feeling like back in the day when I would drive across country from college to home, and when you stopped in a small town, you kind of felt like the guy in the old Bob Seger song "Turn the Page."

I was hardly dressed up, but I had pretty nice shorts on, and a casual short sleeve shirt, but I was dressed up for this crowd. I ordered and sat in the back waiting for my food. I didn't say anything to anyone, but just about each guy at some point just kind of turned around to give me a quick glance. I knew that they knew that I wasn't from around there, and I think they knew that where I was from, there were a whole lot more people. I was a very comfortable intruder in their world.

I actually tried to expand my culinary experience today. When I had plotted this trip out, I really thought I would be eating normally. Not even close. After I got past the absolutely no taste phase, ramen noodles, chocolate shakes, and scrambled eggs were about it, and it was slow going before even those things were even reasonably satisfying.

But things were at least a little better now, and here in Mullen, I ordered a grilled ham and cheese, and a chocolate shake. I hit the road hoping for the best, and at least knowing the chocolate shake would do the trick. The sandwich was OK. It was a little too dry, and the ham was not making the team that much, but I did eat it all. Small victory, but did "note to self," that for the time being I should just go for the grilled cheese. The ham would have to wait.

This whole eating process was weirder for me than it is for most people. I have spent most of my adult life exercising very hard and being a "healthy eater." This started when I gained a lot of weight during college. I have a slow metabolism and can gain weight quite easily. In my early twenties, I was constantly dieting effectively, then gaining it back. I got sick of that and came up with a plan that worked for me. Kind of being on a semi-diet all the time, so that I never had to be on a full-blown one.

Now I *had* to eat, and I needed to gain weight. This might eventually be a little fun, but since ramen noodles currently are far and away my favorite, you can tell I'm not ready to expand my horizons. I'm going to give a thing or two a try on the trip. We'll see.

The Sand Hills of Nebraska are really beautiful. It's like long stretches of the very best parts of the Flint Hills of Kansas, plus the sand part. Driving on Route 2, it was a very peaceful, solitary way to spend the day. You often would go a few minutes without seeing another vehicle. There are almost no trees at all, which created a really cool development as I neared the end of the driving day.

As I was getting closer to the destination of Hot Springs, which is just barely into South Dakota, I turned north onto 385 at Chadron, Nebraska. I had traveled just few miles north, when all of a sudden, in the blink of an eye, a whole slew of magnificent pines appeared, almost like magic. I literally hadn't seen a tree in four hours.

In that blink of an eye, my vista went immediately from high plains rolling landscape to beautiful mountainous views with all of the majestic trees. I virtually was gasping at the panorama. I had been enjoying the hundred-mile vistas you could see in the Sand Hills, but this was something else. I'd get spoiled with all this picturesque landscape in a few days, never growing tired of them, mind you. But the first burst was really something.

Each day of the trip I usually got up and rolled out reasonably early, so it was only late afternoon when I arrived at the Motel 6 in Hot Springs. I was in an area where the communities benefited from Sturgis being in reasonable proximity, added with all of the Black Hills attractions, including Mount Rushmore, which is only 30 miles away. So when I hopped on my bike for a little tour of the town, the first part was on a fairly lengthy stretch of somewhat commercial activity for a small place.

The downtown area was a little bit timeworn, but it had a few things to do. There was always the historic Pioneer Museum, located on a giant bluff high above the town. But when you wandered away from the downtown, at least in this part of the community, it was a lot less "nice small town" than Broken Bow.

There were more trailers than actual houses, and many of them were not in particularly good shape. Of course, being me, it started my mind wandering. As usual, this town was the county seat. I would develop a real knack for picking those towns by accident. About four thousand people live here. It appeared there wasn't much work to be had, and I guess that was reflected in the fairly downtrodden look of the community.

But there must have been an area somewhere I didn't see where the "gentry" of Hot Springs resided. There certainly was plenty of beautiful countryside. There was a small stream that ran alongside the downtown area out toward the north, and it cut through some spectacular red rock formations. It was just one of the commonplace gorgeous views.

Evening came, and on this Saturday night I ventured downtown. I found "The Vault," a bar that seemed to have the most cars parked nearby along the downtown street. It was a nice, spacious place with a very long and ornate bar, and plenty of tables for people to sit and dine. It was about eight o'clock and there were still quite a few families there ahead of the later crowd. The always encouraging sight of a setup for some live music was in view.

There were two waitresses behind the bar and they fit a similar profile. I think that they each fancied themselves kind of sexy. They were rather significantly underdressed, and it appeared that the clothes had been purchased about 30 pounds ago. Either that or they didn't own a mirror, or they really had an admirably distorted sense of their shape.

They acted very flirty in a kind of trashy way, and since I was sitting alone at what otherwise was a crowded bar, I got a lengthy dose of their act—which grew quickly tiring, and actually somewhat pathetic, at least to me. If they were just nice, polite, and efficient I would be having a more conventionally nice evening. But they actually were providing some sort of "burlesquey" entertainment.

Conveniently breaking up the waitress show, and watching the repeat of the day's PGA Tour golf on the TV, two men about my age came in and sat in two adjoining seats. They were very friendly and I soon would learn that they were brothers. One was a pharmacist and the other was in real estate. They clearly didn't live within a few miles of downtown, since I had seen all that. Their wives were down the street playing bingo.

It was great to converse with them. They asked about what brought me to town, and seemed genuinely interested and caring about my situation. I also got to hear all about the area, and they gave me several suggestions of things to see and do, including highly touting their local golf course. I was going to travel tomorrow, so even though tempting, the first golf of the trip would not be in Hot Springs.

They eventually left, and I was fatiguing, but trying to hang in there to hear the live music, which I always enjoy. If it's good, you have discovered a little bit of a treasure. If it's not so good, you admire the effort. If it's really bad, then you get comic relief. The singer-guitarist-piano player finally started up about 10 p.m. He was pretty good, and I admired the fact that he was playing some pretty offbeat stuff that he really liked. They were covers, but by people about everybody in the place wouldn't know. Maybe later he would play the hits, but for now he was playing for himself.

Later wasn't going to happen for me. Each day would be pretty full just like this one, and I had had it about 11. It was back to the Motel 6, and it wasn't long before the second day of this cathartic adventure had ended. It was a wonderful one, and tomorrow beckoned with the promise of Mount Rushmore.

4.

AMERICA THE BEAUTIFUL

May 31, 2015 - Day Three
Hot Springs, South Dakota, to Mount Rushmore to Sheridan, Wyoming - 291 miles

The trip would eventually include only two "touristy" things, and they would come on consecutive days. After what would turn out to be one of the livelier evenings of the journey (and as you found out it wasn't that lively), I was up and ready to roll with both a bike ride and a run. Very nice. Then it was time to make about a 45-minute drive to Mount Rushmore. There was some incredible scenery on the entire trip, but this stretch was perhaps the greatest. I could have stopped and taken a picture about every 3 miles.

Believe it or not, if you're determined to drive three to six hours every day, the amazing landscape actually provided one of the few minor disappointments of the trip. There were so many sights that were worthy of taking a photograph. I only stopped every now and then along the side of the road to take a photo. It was hard because every 20 miles or less provided moments where I would literally look at the landscape and say, "Wow" out loud. It was the heart of the Black Hills, and it was living up to the billing.

On the way north to Mount Rushmore, you can take a route that passes through Sturgis, South Dakota, and I'm sure most people know that it is the community where tens of thousands of motorcycle enthusiasts head for an annual summer gathering. Literally from about a hundred miles away along the various routes that can lead there, the economy is bustling with people stopping, dining and staying over.

When you pass through Sturgis, you get a pretty good idea of what a madhouse it must be in early August during the festival, which is celebrating its 75th annual. Sturgis is only a town of about 7,000, but there are dozens of restaurants and hotel properties there. They certainly picked a wonderful area to have the pilgrimage, since the area is about as scenic as you can possibly get.

Touristy yes, but Mount Rushmore is undeniably spectacular—a must see for all Americans.

I know it is a bit of a cliche going to Mount Rushmore. I have seen the movie where Chevy Chase gazes at an iconic landmark (in that case the Grand Canyon) and he and his family give it a 10-second look, then pack it up and leave. Still, it was pretty damn breathtaking. The sheer magnitude of viewing the four presidents was one thing, but thinking about how this was accomplished with the technology of the day was staggering (construction on the memorial began in 1927, and the presidents' faces were completed between 1934 and 1939—the initial concept called for each president to be depicted from head to waist—but lack of funding forced construction to end in late October 1941). I ended up staying for about 45 minutes, but certainly might have lingered longer if I wasn't traveling so far this day.

Maybe the biggest treat was when I exited the park. There is a sign that says "profile view just ahead." You round the corner, and there is George Washington's profile between a crevasse in the rock face. I had never seen that angle pictured ever before. It, like many views during the entire journey, was spectacular. It just started a head-swiveling day of vistas on the road.

You can take Interstate 90 through this area if you want, but I was not going to do that even if it was faster, and generally on the smaller routes it was pretty smooth going anyway. There was very little traffic, and the road was generally great. It was pretty much uphill from Hot Springs to Mount Rushmore, and the descent through pine forests and river valleys almost defies description.

Then there are the little moments. About an hour outside of Gillette, Wyoming, on Route 14, nature was calling, and I was very thirsty (a recurring theme). Of course I am basically in the middle of nowhere. There is no desperation yet, however, so I just said to myself (and myself was the only person I was speaking with on the trip), "The next place I see is fine." The next place was about 40 miles away.

So in the middle of nowhere, up pops an old gas station, all by its lonesome in Horses Head, Wyoming. There is no gas being sold anymore, but the "Flying A" Amoco sign is still up. It's a bar, it has no name, and there are actually about 15 people hanging around, although none are inside. I ask the lady if I can use her restroom, and she nicely points me in the right direction. After relieving myself, I buy a couple of Cokes to justify my use of the facilities. I just can't believe that this place can do enough business to keep it alive. But there it is.

I did indeed buy Cokes, as in regular Coca-Cola. Before radiation, I hardly touched the real stuff in over 30 years. I long since had switched to Diet Coke, and then about a year ago had stopped drinking soda altogether. On the rare occasion that circumstance had me drink some Coke, the ridiculous syrupy sweetness tasted just awful to me. But post-radiation I needed some sustenance, and since I had almost no taste, that overbearing flavor actually tasted like something, and the carbonation was nice, too. As the pounds fell off, my wife was evangelical about me getting some sugar in my system, and Coke did the trick.

As I noted before, when I made my tentative plan to do this pilgrimage, I did think that I would be completely past the food issues due to my treatments, and that part of my story might include some indigenous food stories. I thought I might spin some tales of county fair corn dogs and the like.

No such luck, I was too optimistic. I was still limited in what my palette was ready for. My taste buds were pretty much back at the start of my trip, but still certain things tasted very metallic, and textures were dicey. Ramen noodles and chocolate shakes still were the standard bill of fare, but as I've said before I was starting to try and branch out.

This particular day I tried a Subway sandwich which somewhat worked OK for lunch, and in the quiet evening in Sheridan I tried to down some pizza ... not a success there. But I'll keep on striving, and soon things will be back to normal. My big joke is that once I can actually eat anything that I want, I will balloon into a fat man. Or not.

The drive in from the lonely outpost Amoco, into Sheridan, was breathtaking. Growing up in New England, there are a considerable amount of pretty rolling areas, and beautiful trees and the like, but even the Green Mountains in Vermont aren't all that high, maybe five thousand feet. I have always loved looking at photos of snowcapped mountains, and really, only a couple of visits to Colorado included that.

So this day was pretty special. The Black Hills at the outset including Mount Rushmore, had eventually given way to some high plains for a while, but toward Sheridan there are incredible views with miles of gorgeous river valleys leading to majestic peaks. Awesome is really not a good enough word for what I was witnessing as afternoon was giving way to evening.

In Hot Springs last night, and Sheridan on this night, I stayed in Motel 6's. Both were fairly new properties, and generally just fine for what I was looking for. But they truly showed how differently run these franchises could be. The towns are pretty similar, Sheridan is certainly a bit bigger, but both rely quite a bit on people traveling on journeys similar to mine.

The Hot Springs motel that was $57.00 per night, had cooperative, friendly people working there, and the slight amenities that you expect at even an economy motel ... i.e., the little soaps and shampoo, etc. The Sheridan Motel 6 was $79.00 per night, and was operated by a grumpy man, who it seemed was employing only members of his family. There was *no* soap, shampoo and the like. I bring some of my own, but it still can be useful. The topper was the sign on the ice machine stating "Be respectful to others, don't fill your ice chest." What a crock. What do people do on long trips? ... uhhhh ... they fill their ice chests.

This Scrooge-like character was clearly trying to squeeze every penny out of his operation. When you book online, which I did in the mornings, they send you a survey afterward asking what you thought of your stay. I pretty much never fill these out, but I sure did on that one. 1 out of 5 across the board, and made some pointed notes in the "comment box."

This was a pretty long day of driving, and much of it was so beautiful and so absorbing that for most of the time I didn't even have the radio on. But there was some time for that, too. I consider myself very fortunate in that I have a real interest and find great joy in a variety of different things.

• • • • •

I mentioned before how much I like listening to the satellite radio channel that features old-time radio shows. I don't really like the comedies like Jack Benny, Bob Hope, and others that much, although it is sometimes interesting to hear what made people laugh a long time ago.

But many of the mystery and detective shows are real favorites. There is one show called "Yours Truly, Johnny

Dollar," which features an insurance investigator that is great. Originally the show would run every weeknight for 15 minutes, but, for the purposes of the satellite channel, they play a full week's episodes, which is one investigation, back-to-back to back. There is a Jim Gaffigan comedy bit where he makes fun of people in old photographs who are sitting in front of the radio, hoping it would become a television. It's a funny skit (he's a very funny guy), but I could definitely have been one of the people in the photograph, and I wouldn't be thinking about needing visuals.

Most readers certainly know the spectacular talents of Orson Welles, at the very least from the movie *Citizen Kane*. He began his career, and became famous by age 21, for his radio work. *War of the Worlds*, of course, is widely known for causing a national crisis from people believing that the Halloween night broadcast was real and that Martians really were invading the Earth.

Welles is all over the channel, and he may be more famous for other things, but he certainly is the greatest radio personality ever, in my humble opinion. Graced with a spectacular speaking voice, he was the original "Shadow." *The Shadow* character would be played by other actors, it is a wonderful detective show, but he was fabulous.

He plays *The Third Man* in the radio series, and he portrayed that character in the movie as well. I could listen to Orson Welles read the phone book, and get a great deal of enjoyment. I don't know if there has ever been a performer who more perfectly fits the "genius" label, and as someone who uses his voice for a living, I am in awe of his talents.

I do feel that for some reason maybe I am someone who

was born at the wrong time, because I also am an over-the-top fan of old movies. Actually I love movies period, and see dozens every year, but the films from the start of the talking era until the start of World War II to me are the best ever made. I can say that I have seen every significant film of that period, since I even like ones like Charlie Chan and Mister Moto, and many of the insignificant shows, too.

I can thank my college days for this particular affection. I took a detective literature course at the University of Kansas as a freshman, and particularly liked the work of Raymond Chandler, best known as the author of *The Big Sleep.* His wonderfully drawn stories of the dark underside of Los Angeles in the thirties and forties just captivated me.

The period captivated me. I misspent many afternoons my freshman year of college skipping class and ... going to the library. I bet you never saw those things in the same sentence before. I would wade into the stacks at Watson Library and dive into "Life" magazines and other period pieces from the 1930s and 1940s. Of course these were all in black and white.

I swear I'm not embellishing the next part. After three or four hours of doing this I went outside to catch the bus back to the dorm. First off, I was rather taken aback that the real world was in color. Secondly, since there were no vehicles except the student busses allowed on the main campus, until one of those modern vehicles came by, I had this distinct feeling that it actually *was* 1940 or something.

It was way back before much cable TV, and Kansas City television station Channel 41 had the entire Warner Brothers catalogue from the 1930s. They used to show old movies starting after the Tonight Show. Many of the movies are not particularly long, so I would fairly often watch two or three until 4 or 5 a.m. This was not especially good for my grades, but it gave me a lifelong passion.

． ． ． ． ．

It was a Sunday night, but Sheridan, Wyoming, was to be, along with Hastings, Nebraska, easily the largest town that I stayed in. But after checking in and showering (using my own toiletries of course), I figured I'd drive around and see what was up. There is a rather lengthy downtown strip in Sheridan, with a lot of nice older buildings and the like.

Maybe it was just this night, maybe it was just every Sunday night in Sheridan, but they had rolled up the streets. Even when I passed a couple of the spots that I looked up online, they were either closed or there was nobody there. I gave it a pretty complete tour of the town before I gave up the ghost, as in ghost town. After the "wild times" in Broken Bow and Hot Springs the past two nights, it was a slight letdown.

But I was once again pretty tired anyway, and it was always nice to just wander back to the motel and wind down, which didn't take much winding. There were great memories to lull me off to sleep, as another solitary, beautiful and thoughtful day had passed.

5.

AGE 8
PINT-SIZED ROCK STAR MOVES ON

By the time I reached the age of 8, I had already moved six times. The first four moves I don't much remember, as my dad, who was carving out a career in radio, bounced from job to job and town to town just about annually. The good thing was that even though he was not leaving each spot on his own volition, his next job was a better one. Since I didn't really know what was going on, this vagabond existence in all likelihood didn't have any real impact on me.

My first clear memory was when I was 4 years old and we were living in Haverhill, Massachusetts. I got stuck up in a tree and my mom had to come and rescue me. My memory is that I was *waaay* up in that tree. I imagine it was probably no more than 10 feet. I guess I am not much for tree climbing because about 10 years later, I was 30 feet up in a tree, and my mom had to call the fire department to rescue me because I couldn't get down.

There are mitigating circumstances to this tale, however. Two of my "friends" were scaling the tree behind me, urging me to go higher. They let me get a few feet above them, and then sawed off the branch I needed to scale back down, leaving me stranded.

Back to the younger days, while I didn't remember the first couple of incidents, I also apparently was on a toddler's crusade to kill my brother Jim, a year my junior. Among other things, I got loose with a paintbrush and a bucket of turpentine when I was two and he was one, and he had to be rushed to the emergency room.

I fully remember what I believe was the last incident of this kind. Apparently, age four was when my full memories started to form, since in Haverhill around the time of the tree incident, I again put poor Jim in peril. We lived in a two-story home, and the way that upper floor was heated was that the heat from downstairs came up through a large steel grate in the floor. Somehow, I managed to get the grate out of its moorings leaving a large hole in the floor/ceiling.

My mother was downstairs in the kitchen preparing for a dinner party. She entered the dining room to finish setting the table and looked up in horror to see that her three-year-old boy was hanging through the hole in the ceiling that he had just walked through. She was able to rescue him before he crashed onto the fine china. My brother and I would not only be close for brothers but as best friends for many years before later estrangement, but those great years of kinship almost didn't come to fruition.

Little Hopkinton rock star with his TV star dad.

The first place of real settlement in my life was Hopkinton, Massachusetts. My dad had become the news director of a radio station in nearby Framingham. That was a much larger town, as I was to find out later. Hopkinton is a typically lovely small New England town with tree-lined streets and the like. It has 14,000 inhabitants these days, and I imagine it might have been half that in the early 1960s when we moved there. It is best known as the starting point of the Boston Marathon.

I was five when we moved into the second floor of a two family home. I already had a brother and a sister, and would have two more brothers added in the three years plus that we lived there. As the oldest, I received advantages that probably weren't warranted or fair to my siblings, but since I was the first, I would reach the age for things before the others, like kindergarten.

There was no public kindergarten in the town, heck there was none anywhere. But I went to a private kindergarten each day, just the start of me developing into a little bitty rock star in this small town. I was a good student, I loved to read, and I had a great thirst for knowledge of just about everything.

The town library had a children's section, and by the time I was midway through second grade, much to my chagrin, I had read every single book in the children's section. They actually expanded their catalogue due to this. At this time I was kind of splitting time between second and third grade curriculum. The previous year in first grade, when asked to spell out an English sentence on the board, I wrote it in cursive. The teacher informed me that none of the other children could read cursive, to which I replied, "Well, that's their problem." It's a good thing that otherwise I was considered a nice young boy, because I had an annoying wealth of confidence.

Being a big fish in this small pond played itself out in sports, too. I had been a very enthusiastic baseball player from the time that my dad started tossing a ball with me at age three. By the time that organized play was to begin in Midget League, the level below Little League, I was ready to roll. While Hopkinton was a little town, they had a very well organized baseball operation. The Midget games were Friday evenings at a beautifully maintained field. There was even a public address announcer. I was better than most my first year, and my age 8 year, I was the best.

When you were the star player, you had to alternate games as a position player and pitcher because you were only allowed to pitch every other game. The local newspaper sponsored an award that gave any player who pitched a no-hitter or hit a home run a free hot dog and soda. I achieved this "feat" in every single game that season. As you might imagine, it's not as "amazing" as it sounds. If you could throw strikes and had a good arm, whiffing little guys who were mostly afraid of the ball was not too hard. As far as the homers, if you hit the ball into the outfield, it generally rolled through or past the outfielders for an easy tour of the bases.

But that still didn't mean that my dad wasn't proud as a peach. My picture was taken by the newspaper each week noting my feat. It also created an interesting weekly "lapse of memory" by Dad. I was Catholic, and of course it was Friday, and not eating meat was even more of a sin back then than it is today. But I would get my hot dog, and until I was about halfway through the big prize treat, my dad would conveniently not remember it was Friday. He then would say that it was OK to finish.

This might be a good time to urge anyone of my generation who was raised Catholic to find the fantastic comedy album "Class Clown" by George Carlin, which came out in the 1970s. One entire side is about the vagaries and absurdities of some of the rules and tenets of the Catholic Church at the time. It is hysterical, but as Carlin always managed, it carried a good deal of common sense. His world view and mine aren't too far different, and he was one of the few celebrities I was truly saddened to lose when he died a few years ago.

The baseball season ended pretty early in the summer, which was a good thing, seeing as I would not have completed the season, since it was time for us to move again. The reason for the move was a very good one, although it would mean leaving the place that had provided the first stability in my life, and where I had thrived. My dad received the first big break of his career. He had moved from his news director's job in Framingham to a job as a news writer at WBZ-TV in Boston a year earlier.

A friend at the station urged him to audition when a weekend news anchor spot opened up, and having never done television before, he got the job. I have a very fond memory of my mother excitedly getting lunch made early so we could sit on the floor in front of our black and white TV and watch the Saturday noon news. He obviously did well since it was not very long after that he got the big job on the 6 and 11 p.m. news on weekdays.

That meant a significant raise, and the decision to move to a nice suburban house in Framingham, the home that my parents still live in. It was high times; we bought a new car, too, a big station wagon needed to truck around five children. To show

how the world has changed in 50 years, I still remember it being explained to me that a good rule of thumb for purchasing a house was to buy one about as expensive as the salary you made. My dad was making $25,000, so they bought a $25,000 house.

Can you imagine someone today thinking that they had to make $300,000 per year to buy a home at that price? Heck, there might not be a single American who follows that stream of logic by even half. Of course, the home that my parents bought is now worth more than the $300,000. There was a very large backyard, and a wooded area that was part of the property as well. It was a very nice place to grow up.

But the growing up part was going to be quite a bit different. In Hopkinton, I was on the verge of being double promoted. Framingham was a much larger town, probably 60,000 people when we moved there. I'm not going to say it was culture shock, and I initially made a very good adjustment, but it was certainly a greater challenge in all of the areas that had come so easy to me before.

The elementary school that I went to for third grade was probably three times the size of the one in Hopkinton, even though that was the *only* one in town. There were probably eight or ten in Framingham. But I was still one of the better students in class, leading the pack in the SRA reading competition. It's so funny/sad thinking back to what was considered good learning incentive at that time in the mid-1960s.

That SRA deal included motivations to move up the ladder by color-coding and you also got stars on a chart that showed how much and how well you had read. Those were posted in the class, which of course was fine for a good reader, but how about the kids who were struggling a bit? They were basically being shamed as their charts were barren of stars, while those of us blessed to read easily could barely fit them.

Worse yet, there were two levels, clearly defined for "Fast Readers" and "Slow Readers." Nice esteem building, huh? Perhaps if you are a bit old school you might think of this as good, solid competition. I think of it more in terms of the "lesser" students, and that they could have found a better way of encouragement.

I guess the only other major adjustment was more comic. Apparently, the move to the big town, and the third grade meant that the girls got more aggressive. Even at that young age, I secretly liked girls, but not *all* of them. The first day that school ended, a girl I didn't find all that fetching named Mary Ellen started chasing after me as soon as we walked out the door. I didn't want to be caught by her, and I was decidedly faster.

She was a persistent gal and the roundabout way that I had to go home, even though a straight shot to my house was about six hundred yards, was probably three-quarters of a mile. She gamely chased me all the way to the point I turned onto my dead end street cul-de-sac. This was repeated for about three weeks before she finally gave up the quest. I don't quite know what I was running from, but I got home fast every day. Perhaps this was a precursor of my running days many years hence.

The home I ran to was where I would live all the years until I went to college. It was a nice home, and a nice neighborhood, lots and lots of children around. Before my mom laid down the law, we had yet another addition to our family, my youngest sister Colleen. I wasn't even 10 when she arrived, making it six children in less than a decade. I only mention this because in our cul-de-sac, basically all the families were Catholic or Jewish. The Jewish families mostly had two children, one had three. Our six were the *fewest* children of any of the Catholic families, one of them topping out at 13. No shortage of candidates for hide-and-seek.

My childhood vagabond days were over. 11 Brookvale Road in Framingham was the always busy, always noisy, mainly loving home for the duration of my childhood. Room for baseball and football in the backyard, and lots of woods for wild adventures, or at least we thought they were wild.

I often am thankful that we did move from Hopkinton. I think things would have come too easy for me in the little town I was grabbing by the throat. I would need the challenges, and the failure, and the comedowns to drop me down the several pegs I think I would need to be taken. I believe I would have been quite a piece of work otherwise.

6.

Epic Storms and Attack Chickens

June 1, 2015 - Day Four
Sheridan, Wyoming to Little Bighorn Battlefield, Montana
to Belle Fourche, South Dakota - 285 miles

After the very quiet Sunday evening in Sheridan, it was up early at my penny-pinching Motel 6, and out for a great bike ride. The motel was up near the highway, rather high above the town. Down the hill I went, knowing that the end of the ride was going to be some serious working out going back uphill. As I have noted before, there is a rather wide dichotomy in the smallish towns about how people live in their modest homes. Here in Sheridan, it was a slight economic step-up from Hot Springs, South Dakota, where all of the nicer neighborhoods must have been on the outskirts of town. Sheridan featured one spot where there was a lovely home at the end of the street, well maintained with a 1960s "My Three Sons" feel. Directly across the small street was a ramshackle, run down home fenced in with chicken wire, complete with overgrown weeds, bare dirt, and old appliances ... the whole 9 yards (or one crummy yard). On the fence, there was a sign warning passersbys to beware of "Attack Chickens." I don't think it was a joke.

In all of these towns, I thought of how the people with the nice homes dealt with (or didn't) their careless neighbors. I had a mental picture of a contentious town council meeting with Mr. Jones berating Mr. Smith about the condition of his abode, and the effect that it had on their little neighborhood. Nothing seems to come of it, though.

As I have noted before, I never really formed a travel plan before the day arrived. Today was kind of a combination of not any plan at all and some overall thoughts that I might have formed previously. It would be an ambitious day where I would cover more than my share of bases.

There had been only three states in the union where I had never been. Now that isn't quite as impressive as it might seem, since some of them I had only passed through or just been in an airport there. Washington and Washington D.C. both fit that bill. I have passed through Seattle three times on my way to Alaska for the Great Alaska Shootout basketball tournament. A bucket list item still exists for our nation's capital, since I have only seen the monuments while landing in the D.C. airport, either laying over, or going to Baltimore.

The three remaining states were Oregon, Idaho, and Montana. Seeing as I was just a few miles away from Montana, I thought I might as well scratch that one off. So after the nice final climb up the slope on the bicycle ride today and back to the Motel 6, I cooled off with my trusty little map and my laptop.

I obviously was close to the point where I could comfortably turn around and head back toward home. I knew that I was only about four hours away from Yellowstone, but that would mean eight hours back and forth added driving, and I didn't want to be in rush-mode late in the week. So I decided that the west-

Vistas like this were what I had dreamed of during my radiation treatment—Sheridan, Wyoming, is spectacular.

ern-most outpost of the journey would be the Little Bighorn Battlefield National Monument at Crow Agency, Montana.

I am a very big fan of history. Actually, I unofficially minored in it in college. I took seven history courses adding up to 21 hours, and was going to take yet another my senior year. I was taking a very heavy course load and needed every credit, and my adviser told me that I could take the course, but it wouldn't count toward graduation. I had maxed out on history. I took an extremely boring accounting course instead.

So today, the opportunity to soak in a little history, see some more wonderful landscape, and get my "states visited" list down to two combined for great incentives. The long day included a properly somber visit to Little Bighorn, an extensive drive through Montana and South Dakota, and for good measure, the first round of golf of the trip.

Leaving Sheridan behind, it was only an hour or so to Little

Bighorn. I am either ¼ or ¹/₈ Native American. The family history on my father's side is somewhat murky, but either way, visiting the site would have some emotion to it. I also have read a considerable amount about the rather absurd legend of General George Custer. He had a fairly distinguished career with more than its share of controversies, and certainly the depiction of him as a tragic victim in his final battle seems well overdone.

Leaving that argument to other more learned folk, I still found it was very much a worthwhile stop in beautiful Black Hills country. There is plenty of wide-open space after making the turn east on state route 212, and shortly thereafter, you get to the Battlefield Monument and Museum.

I haven't visited that many battlefields, but when I have, I am often struck by how brutal warfare really is. There is nothing here around Little Bighorn but open ground gently rising to a point probably no higher than one hundred feet above the rest of the terrain.

It certainly didn't look like any wise spot to me to make a "Last Stand." The higher ground didn't provide much advantage. The other jarring part was that anyone certainly could have clearly seen if there was a serious numerical disadvantage, which of course Custer had. A complete slaughter seems like no surprise to me.

A somber feeling enveloped me as I walked around. First of all, it's a gigantic cemetery with row after row of white crosses. Many soldiers are buried here from other battles besides this one. When you go on top of the hill to the original burial ground, it is noted that they really couldn't identify most of the U.S. military victims found there. They just guessed from the list of soldiers in the company.

Even in a rout, many of the "victors" are also victims. There is a finely crafted monument to the Native Americans lost as well. There is certainly a radical dichotomy of the absolutely beautiful countryside with the mountains in the distance, and the carnage that took place here. It also sinks in that there are thousands of these places all around the world.

I have made it a point since my treatment to not just let moments pass, but to truly let things sink in. I want to stick to that over and over. I can be pretty matter-of-fact about things. I have covered thousands of games, but that shouldn't mute the enjoyment of true greatness. One of the reasons for the route that I took on this trip was the beauty that I knew was out there, and the time was right to enjoy it as much as I ever would have.

The battlefield was a very valuable experience, but now it was time to get back on the road. I would drive the final 200 miles through southeastern Montana, through just a touch of Wyoming, and into South Dakota on Route 212. Anyone looking for solitude, and certainly that was a big part of the agenda, would find this road was for them. It was gorgeous. The road meandered through river valleys with red rock outcroppings on either side.

The speed limit was 80, which meant you could comfortably cruise from 85-87 mph, although I will say that is about the upper edge of my courage level. But since there was nobody on the road, it didn't feel dangerous. It was mostly just a two-lane road, but you would often travel for five minutes at a time without seeing another vehicle. I had also not seen a police car anywhere but a construction zone since I left Broken Bow. Of course, while sweeping my head back and forth taking in the

At Little Bighorn. If I had a hat like this before — sun protection — I wouldn't have needed to take the trip.

scenery, I might have missed a few.

The landscape in this area was just wonderful. It wasn't the epic mountains like around Sheridan, Wyoming, but instead river valleys with high bluffs of red rock rising above them. Since there were often no vehicles in sight, it was like driving through a western movie landscape. I would have been much more suited to be riding a horse.

This morning I had selected Belle Fourche, South Dakota, as the day's destination. It fit into the distance that I wanted to drive each day, and I could arrive in the middle of the afternoon. Scouting for my first golf course of the trip, Belle Fourche Country Club seemed like a nice, scenic, economical choice.

After the beautiful drive, I arrived at the Econo Lodge at 2:30. It was a clean, simple property with a very nice man at the front desk running the operation. I knew the golf course was pretty close, but it was a little embarrassing to ask the guy where it was and have him walk out the front door, point, and say, "right over there."

I changed into my golf stuff and went over to the course. I was told that I had about 90 minutes to get nine holes in and get back out for another nine because it was Husbands and Wives League night. It was a nine-hole golf course on a very hilly piece of property and extremely beautiful. It wasn't the greatest course, but it was in nice shape and on a sunny, late afternoon with thunderstorms bubbling up, creating mountainous cloud formations all around—it was quite awesome.

I would play three rounds of golf on the trip, and from the standpoint of my execution, they were all the same. I can be a master of pretty much making the highest score possible out of the quality of my play. At Belle Fourche, I probably should have

The front of my score card from the Belle Fourche Country Club.

shot about 79, but instead finished with an 84. But in this circumstance, I did a pretty good job of not letting it bother me as
much as usual.

After I was done, I sat on the little patio, had a beer,
and watched the husbands and wives tee off. They were all
extremely happy just to be out for some fun including beverages, and didn't care very much that most of their shots went
awry. It was a nice small town scene.

The thunderstorms did come through and they were some
beauties. I always hope that I won't later hear of anything
bad happening out of the storms, since I love watching them.
This was a pretty good light show, and of course living in the
Midwest, we get to see a lot of them. The most spectacular
storm of that kind I ever saw, however, and it's not close, was
not in the United States. It was in Puerto Vallarta, Mexico.

My wife and I have visited there a couple of times, but

on this particular visit, we got a great deal on our hotel suite because it was the last week before the autumn busy season. We found out why. The first couple of days were paralyzingly hot and humid. We went for a walk downtown one day, and because we slipped into a couple of jewelry stores merely because they had air conditioning, my wife has a couple of hundred dollars of jewelry she wouldn't have otherwise.

We had arrived on a Saturday and it wasn't until Monday night that relief finally arrived about 10 p.m. when a vicious thunderstorm roared through. Our hotel room was about 10 floors up with a covered deck which faced away from the ocean and a view toward the mountainside where homes seemed to be literally waiting to topple down into the sea.

The rain came down so hard it was difficult to see those homes, but they were repeatedly illuminated by lightning strikes that came about every half second. It looked like an old historic film I'd seen of the Battle of Britain. It was utterly fantastic, maybe five times more explosive than any other thunderstorm I have ever seen.

We awoke the next morning to beautiful sunshine and warm, not blistering hot, weather. Amazingly, all those expensive homes were still hanging on the hillside, and somehow, all of the rainwater was just gone, disappearing into the sandy soil and the ocean itself.

· · · · ·

The Belle Fourche thunderstorm version was pretty good though, and over in about an hour. I went out for a drive to see what was going on, which was nothing. Belle Fourche seemed like a very nice town with a nicely-lit baseball complex where the night's games had been washed out. It appeared that there might be a little fun to be had if not for the fact that it was a Monday night, and it had just rained like hell.

I stopped at a restaurant/bar which was quite an expansive place with a couple of rooms. There was a Cardinals game on all of the televisions. I played a game of Golden Tee golf. I'm good enough at it to have some fun and be competitive in the online contests, about half the time winning something that makes a future game a little cheaper. I am not, however, one of the super-crazy folks who must play all the time and know the little tricks that can allow you to shoot 24 under or something.

I find the game a pleasant diversion occasionally, when I am somewhere by myself and there isn't much going on or there isn't a game on television that I am riveted to. That kind of fit tonight. I finished Golden Tee after playing one game and then sat at the bar for a few minutes. It was only about 9 o'clock, but this was, and would prove to be, my busiest day of the trip, and I was about cashed in.

I went back to the motel, and as I did most nights, if I could keep my eyes open, made a few notes about the day. It had been an excellent and varied day. I experienced attack chickens to far more important thoughts of a historic real attack with real consequences. There was the jarring juxtaposition of a mean-spirited motel operator to a more typically nice American small-business owner, proud of his motel. I saw sunshine and thunderstorms, the joys of golf for all skill levels, and more.

I had only been able to hope that the days on my trip would be so full and satisfying, and they had. Today was so jam-packed that once again I went from reviewing the day's pleasures to dreaming about them, dead asleep, in the blink of an eye.

7.

WAITING FOR IMPACT

June 2, 2015 - Day 5
Belle Fourche, South Dakota to Murdo, South Dakota - 190 miles

I woke up to another sunny and beautiful day in this nice little town. I could virtually tour the entire community on my bike. There were a couple of lovely city parks, and one big difference. Hockey rinks instead of basketball or tennis courts were a common sight.

Of course, it was June, and even here the ice was long gone. I assume that they play what we used to call street hockey, that was played just running around. Or perhaps they played roller hockey, which we never did. But it did make me think of playing river hockey back in Massachusetts when I was a kid. It's all a bit more organized here.

Hockey exploded in Boston right around 1970, which I will go into a little later. Anyone who played sports played hockey. More ambitious folks would pack down snow in their yards and build snowbanks and then put down water and concoct makeshift rinks, but most of us played on the river.

We weren't guys just with a pair of skates and a stick. We had way more gear than that. Common Christmas gifts in my early teens for me and a lot of my friends were hockey gloves, shin pads, and socks. Our parents also bought us helmets, but this was still the era when hardly any pros wore a helmet, so down at the river you could watch 15 guys playing pickup hockey, with 15 helmets laying by the shore.

Our neighborhood area group played in a cove on the Sudbury River. The cove would freeze solid pretty quickly in the winter, but it was a big river, and it seldom froze solid out toward the middle. When it did, it was the most glorious surface ever. Black Ice, we called it, because it was thick enough to skate on, but you could still see through it. It was slick and speedy, much more so that the milky white, thicker, and yes, safer ice was near the shore. Most of the time however, eventually the ice that could support us enough for a game gave way to flowing river.

This created a daily phenomenon due to the fact that one goal in the makeshift rink backed up the shore, and the other had the open river far behind it. But not miles behind it. We generally had a "no lifting" rule, meaning you had to keep the puck on the ice except on the rare occasions when both teams had a kid with goaltending gear. In either case, some of the shots that missed the net, and went through our snow barrier, skittered out into water, or onto ice too thin to skate on and retrieve.

On many days we ran out of pucks, but we still wanted to play, and there would be a couple out on the thin ice. Youthful stupidity taking over, we would draw straws to see who would be the guy who went out on his belly (to distribute the weight, we thought) to retrieve a last puck or two. Nobody ever went through the ice out there where the water was probably 30 feet deep, but it certainly could have happened.

Riding around through Belle Fourche and seeing the multiple outdoor rinks also made me think of all of the hockey games I have broadcast through the years. It kind of started as a kid when I would roll game after game of Bobby Orr and the Boston Bruins into my reel-to-reel tape recorder as I watched the games on TV.

Bobby Orr of the Bruins is the greatest athlete I have ever watched, and I'm not so sure it's close. He is the rarest of breeds, someone who truly changed the way a game is played. Like Babe Ruth, who changed baseball from a slap hitting, run and steal sport, to power hitting, Orr was a defenseman, and he would once lead the league in scoring. If you had asked any hockey fan before he came along if that could happen, they would have looked at you like you had two heads.

I won't write a chapter on Bobby Orr and his otherworldly talents, but merely a paragraph. When the puck was left behind the net by the Bruins goalie, the whole Boston Garden would rise, because there was a good chance that Orr was going to take it coast-to-coast through a whole team and score or assist. He once killed off an entire penalty by himself. The Bruins won the faceoff, gave it to him, and he skated around and away from the Los Angeles Kings for the full two minutes. Watch some clips on YouTube sometime. You won't be disappointed.

Every sport has its challenges for a play-by-play announcer, but as far as calling the game, hockey is *easily* the most difficult. If you can master hockey you can pretty much do anything. I was the voice of Colgate University for a couple of years in the late 1980s. Colgate is in the ECAC, one of just six Division One hockey conferences.

The difficulty of the sport is pretty evident. The players don't play more than a couple of minutes at a time, and shuttle in and out. Hockey sweaters also don't have numbers on the front. This was made more of an issue in the ECAC. Almost every arena was a fieldhouse style building, usually holding about 3-4,000 rabid fans. Almost all of them also had the press box on one end. So half the action was a couple of hundred feet away, and then when players were skating toward you, it was the front of the jersey you saw. It took some work, but I loved it. I very much enjoyed getting to do it again for the Missouri Mavericks recently.

The ECAC was a very enjoyable assignment, but it had some real challenges. The travel could be dicey. I drove everywhere in the league which had several schools in upstate New York, and a few in New England. The Ivy League did not have their own separate league, and their hockey playing schools were in the ECAC. Most of the schools in the league were fine academic institutions, set in beautiful, small northeast college towns.

The other team in the league was Army, which certainly fit the profile. West Point is a beautiful place in a very picturesque area. However, my lone road trip to West Point almost resulted in you not reading this book, because I wouldn't have been around to write it. It is normally a gorgeous drive from Utica, New York, where I was working, to West Point, and it was actually very pretty as I drove down there. But part of that was the heavy snow that began to fall.

The driving was getting more treacherous as I drew closer to West Point. I was supposed to get there in time to do my 4:20 p.m. sportscast. I stopped at a gas station about 50 miles away to use the pay phone to tell the folks back at the station that I was going to be able to get there. But conditions worsened. I had a front wheel drive car, so it was pretty good in the snow. I reached a steep hill just outside of West Point, and cars were sliding backward down the hill past me. It was a slow motion preview of white-knuckle moments to come.

I actually did make it, but not at 4:20. I set up my gear by about 5:00 and dialed in. The only time I have ever cursed in anger at a co-worker came when the news director asked me where the hell I had been for my first sportscast. Having just risked my life to get there, I told him to fuck off, and went on about my business.

I did the game, and now the trick was to get home. It was usually about a three-hour drive, but it had been snowing since mid afternoon. If it was today, I wouldn't have thought twice and never had made the drive. But I didn't make much money, and I likely wouldn't have been reimbursed for the motel. In addition to that, if you live in upstate New York, you get so used to it snowing you kind of just become numb to it.

It was slow going on I-90, but we were at least going. Experienced snow drivers knew that if you kept a steady pace and didn't hit the brakes unless absolutely necessary, you could maintain maybe 45 mph even on the snow packed road in the blinding blizzard. Unfortunately, all it takes is one panicky driver to slam the brakes to cause disaster ... which is just what happened.

One person up ahead apparently felt a slight slippage and hit the brakes and started spinning. This caused a chain reaction in the line of cars behind it, and soon cars were sliding all over the road, and now you had to try and brake. I did, with the predictable results. I started spinning like a top, and after 540 degrees my car came to a stop facing backward right smack in the middle of the road.

I looked up to see perhaps only 200 yards up the road the headlights of two semis side-by-side coming right for me. There was no time to do anything, so I buried my head in my hands, flopped down on the seat, and waited for impact, basically hoping that when the car got smashed, I might somehow survive it.

The highway had guardrails almost all of the way in the hilly area for safety so there was nowhere to swerve, but for some reason in this little stretch there weren't any. Seconds later, I heard horns blaring, and I felt a gigantic whoosh so strong it actually blew my car a pretty good bit down the road. Each truck had managed to swerve out of each of the two lanes and just barely get around, not hitting me, but blowing me down the road.

It was pretty much a miracle, but I didn't have much time to think about that. I quickly restarted the stalled car, and got the hell down the road. I soon had passed the worst of the snow, and moved on back home. All those drives through the northeast in the winter have made me hate winter driving since, but I am good at it, from vast experience.

The ECAC play-by-play assignment did have one very disappointing moment from a professional standpoint. The last year that I did the Colgate University games, they were the best team in the league in the regular season. Eight teams made the postseason conference tournament, and the first round series were on campus sites of the higher seed, and then the four winners would advance to the Boston Garden for the semifinals and finals.

It was with great anticipation I hoped to go to Boston and the historic Garden to broadcast the games. All the Celtics and Bruins games I watched and attended through the years, with the banners hanging from the rafters of the old building, and now I was going to get to live a real dream by working there.

Well, the Red Raiders went out and became the first ever #1 seed in ECAC history to lose their first round series on home ice. No Boston Garden dream scenario for me. The next year our radio station gained the rights to the New Jersey Devils AHL team, and we did those games and had to drop Colgate. I never would broadcast a game at Boston Garden.

.   .   .   .   .

My morning bike ride this day was one of the more pleasant. The lovely parks and nice neighborhoods of Belle Fourche were combined with the lively business district. It seems to be a very nice place to live. I mentioned earlier on the first day of my trip that I stopped in Lebanon, Kansas, to take a picture as it is the geographical center of the country. It turns out that it's the center of the contiguous U.S. When you include Alaska and Hawaii, the geographical center is ... 20 miles north of Belle Fourche. How about me, being in both of them within four days?

Of course, Belle Fourche seems a lovely place to live when it's early June. As I started off the day's journey, I would get another indication of what winter life was like here. I have never driven in the winter in this area of the country. I have been previously to North and South Dakota to broadcast basketball games, and on one of the trips experienced minus 34 degree weather (not wind chill either), but when you drive east on I-90 I saw signs that gave a real hint as to the challenges of a Dakota winter.

Periodically a large sign with light standards affixed would say, "When lights flashing I-90 closed, go back to previous exits." Wouldn't that be dandy? There is no other way to get anywhere, you would just be stuck. Nice for the motel business I guess, and not much else. The couple of hours on I-90 were among the limited time I spent on interstates, but you are generally in such remote areas it doesn't seem like it. Still, I preferred the back roads.

I had driven at least five hours a day so far on the trip and wanted to start to tone that down, so I searched out a location not quite so far, and came up with Murdo, South Dakota. I hit the road and flipped the radio on, and turned to the old-time radio channel. I wasn't much paying attention to dates, but it would become quickly evident that D-Day was approaching.

The station was replaying a broadcast of live news reports of the Normandy invasion. It was fascinating, and my thoughts were a combination of great admiration for the valor of those who hit the beach, and melancholy similar to the feelings I had only two days before at the Little Bighorn battlefield. The situations surrounding the two events were certainly completely different, but one thing was the same—young men wading into slaughter.

If I had known just how remote the outpost I had chosen was, Murdo might not have been on the agenda. But it would have its own share of quirks and interesting people and events.

I checked into the very economical American Inn Motel. It touted a swimming pool, which sounded nice on a blistering hot day, and I looked forward to using it after playing some golf outside of town. I received my giant metal room key and dropped my stuff into my extremely Spartan digs, and then I checked out the pool. It was June and it was hot, but there would be no swimming. The pool was empty, and it kind of looked like it might have been quite a few years since it hadn't been.

But there was golf to be had. So I jumped in the car and drove a couple of miles out of town to the Murdo Golf Club. There was no one to be found on this giant area of prairie. I walked into the pro shop, still saw nobody, but the sign said "Open," and the door certainly was, so I went out and found the cart barn. Still no one, but there were carts with keys in them, so I loaded my clubs on one, figuring I could pay later.

As I drove toward what I had guessed was the first tee box, finally a lone figure came running at me, waving a cowboy hat, and he directed me to the pro shop again. I felt better about being "legal" now, and paid him the $30 to play 18 holes.

There was an untold amount of mosquitoes flying around. I had about a quart of bug spray on, but this was a Normandy Invasion of mosquitoes. As I addressed the ball for my second shot, I looked down at my legs and saw about 30 mosquitoes on each leg digging in. I brushed them off, looked around, and saw a father and son, the only other people on the course. I drove my cart over and asked if there was any relief on other portions of the course. No, was the answer, and they were about to quit, too.

The proprietor was gracious and returned my money noting that there must have been a good mating season for the little pests. He was certainly right about that. It was a little bit disappointing, but it was a wise decision and I only had to suffer with a handful of bites.

It was late afternoon on this steamy South Dakota day, and I soaked up some air conditioning in the car, drove around for a bit, then went back to the hotel, and took a shower, planning on maybe picking up a bite to eat or grab a beer at some tiny local haunt. A drive around revealed quickly that there was no local haunt.

It was many miles to any other towns, and they were smaller still than Murdo. While I like to have a little evening distraction, there would be nothing wrong after several days on the road to enjoy some quietude in the not so swanky confines of the American Inn Motel.

I really enjoy staying in hotels and motels of all shapes and sizes, and I like very nice ones that have a great gym, a beautiful lap pool, and an ornate lobby. But there is something to be said for balancing that luxury with a dose of a one-queen bed, TV bolted to the wall up high, bed sheet quality shower curtain abode as well. In these humble surroundings, I settled in with a Robert B. Parker mystery, and read myself to sleep.

Nice.

8

AGE 11
WHIPSMART INSPIRATION

It might seem a little strange that possibly the most defining year of a person who is middle-aged occurred when he was 11. But there is no question that many of the events, the people, and the atmosphere of this time at the end of my elementary school years shaped my outlook on life. Also, there is little question that the last year of my life, and some of the decisions that I made regarding the approach looking to get past my cancer treatment, were rooted in this year.

Summer was winding down, and it had been a typical American summer for a suburban kid of that place and time. I played baseball, but that wasn't the kind of all consuming thing that we see now, even for a good player. We played 18 games, two games a week for nine weeks, and I missed two of those to take our normal vacation at the regular time.

My dad was in one of the periods where the TV profession was treating him kindly. We annually would rent a house on Little Ossippee Lake in New Hampshire. It was only about 20 miles away from Old Orchard Beach, Maine. So our days would be a delightful mix of swimming and boating on the lake in the morning, and riding the oceans waves and lying in the sun in the afternoon.

Besides that, most of the time my brother Jim and I, and our friends would play baseball or whiffle ball for hours on end, or march around in the woods surrounding our home and pretend we were on big adventures. Sometimes we would "camp out" in tents in the woods, although we were no more than a quarter of a mile from all of our homes.

One of the vivid memories was how many stars you could see when it got pitch dark at 2 or 3 a.m. and you would be lying on your back and staring up into the sky. A less idyllic memory was when we were roasting marshmallows over an open fire and my brother's marshmallow caught fire. He panicked and flung it, and the burning confection seared sticky goo and sweatshirt to my arm.

August bled into September and it was time to start the sixth grade. My first concern was that the convenient summer buzz cut hadn't grown sufficiently. This was 1967, not that we were hippies, but at the very least you wanted to have your hair the length of Davy Jones of the Monkees. It wasn't, but hair grows.

The first day of school is always very exciting, but this first day was more important than most. In walked our teacher. Miss Rubinwitch. She was a lovely dark haired lady in a minidress. Lady is perhaps stretching it a bit, and by that I mean this was her first teaching job. She was 22 years old, and I don't even really know how to describe what I thought. Smitten I guess at the least.

She was smart, bubbly, and enthusiastic. I was the stereo-typical smartest kind in the class, but I also liked to have fun. That dynamic was going to go a long way toward forging our relationship, which lasts until this day.

You see, when you are the smart kid, but also the class clown, the teacher has a tough job. First of all, being a class clown is pretty easy work. All you have to do is be reasonably clever, and have the guts to interrupt the proceedings with your pithy comments. And the best way to get away with it is to make the teacher laugh, too.

But the teacher also has to have control of the proceedings, so Miss Rubinwitch would sometimes have to dole out some sort of punishment for my disruptions. That usually meant I had to stay after school and clean the erasers and such. Horrible punishment, huh? More time with the whipsmart and lovely brunette with the long legs and lovely figure, barely a decade older than the kid uneasily moving into puberty.

But this was more than an adolescent crush. I respected and admired Miss Rubinwitch, and she felt rightly or wrongly that she could inspire a kid with plenty of brains, and not a heckuva lot of direction. I wasn't your normal 11-year-old. Yeah, I liked baseball and girls, but my favorite TV show was the *CBS Evening News*, and I had been reading the news and editorial section of the paper since I was five.

Miss Rubinwitch had been very active in college in the civil rights movement and had done the March on Washington and seen Martin Luther King's "I Have a Dream" speech. So staying after school and clapping the erasers, and soon helping her grade papers, I got to hear a lot about that. I had long conversations about issues that I came to care very greatly about. She was definitely inspiring me.

I didn't realize it at the time, but she surely was one of the major reasons that I have been almost the opposite of a chauvinist. I am the type of guy whose head is on a swivel when it comes to looking at ladies, but that doesn't have any effect on what I think of them as co-workers, leaders, and business people.

I have always cringed when conversations turn in the

"dumb blonde" direction. There's plenty of stupidity for both sexes to evenly share. Even worse is when guys go on and on complaining about their wives. My answer is simple, if you hate it so much, don't get or stay married. Relationships aren't perfect, but they ought to be good.

Miss Rubinwitch and I did things that you could never do today, and I don't mean anything close to tawdry, just stuff that would be frowned on big time. When I finished my "punishment" after school, she would often drive me home in her convertible. My house wasn't very far away at all, but I sure as hell took the ride.

I helped her move from one apartment to another, and I helped paint that new apartment. Sometimes my best friend Tommy, who was in the class, would be along, but mostly it was just me and Miss Rubinwitch. I made the same grades I usually did in school, straight A's with the usual C- for "self-control," but I also got to do extra assignments she would assign to challenge me.

One of those was when she gave me and the smartest girl in the class the opportunity to write a research paper on the history topic of our choice. I don't know if some students would be thrilled that the reward for the best two history students in the class was more work, but I was.

I chose the Russian Revolution for my topic. I had an advantage over my fellow "winner." My dad would take me and my brother Jim to work at his radio and television station most Saturdays and Sundays. Not only did we have hours to read the wire service copy, and run football film through an editing viewfinder, I had plenty of time to research my paper without any distractions.

This will no doubt make many people either laugh or scratch their heads, but the other advantage was that the station had the latest electronic typewriters. We were on a deadline of three weeks I think, and this really helped. I believe that the girl would face the challenge of turning in the paper in longhand.

This type of competition probably wasn't the best idea, but I not only reveled in it, I was inspired to impress my teacher. When the time came, I had churned out a 21 page, typewritten epic on the revolution that I probably should have kept, because I took a Russian Revolution class in college, and I bet that thing would have gotten me an A at KU.

I was proud as a peach when it was time for us to turn the paper in, in front of the class. I don't know whether the girl was overwhelmed or knew that I was going to go to the ends of the earth to produce a good product, but she showed up with nothing. She was really a nice shy kid, and it clearly was very embarrassing for her. Actually, it kind of killed my fun. I felt bad for her, and I couldn't much enjoy my prideful "victory"

And if you think that events through ones youth stick forever, think about this. I didn't share many classes with that girl through the years, but we went to the same schools, and we graduated from the same high school.

At my 15th high school reunion, a girl that I knew asked me if I would dance with this girl, because she wasn't having a good time. I said sure, and the first fast dance ended and morphed into a slow dance. I thought it would be bad form to stop then, so on we went to the awkward, slow, second dance.

The song was long enough for her to not only mention that she still was embarrassed about not turning in that paper, but she also launched into a bitter diatribe about all of the "popular girls" from high school, and how things never change. She had become a very successful businesswoman by this point, but on this night she could care less. Those youthful slights clearly still burned deeply.

It was a wonderful school year that saw 1967 become 1968. But as we drew closer to the end of this school year, two things happened that really changed me as a person. First, in April I was listening to my transistor radio and they came on with a bulletin that Martin Luther King, Jr. had been shot and killed in Memphis. Having spent the year hearing stories about his famous speech, this really shook me up.

The subsequent racial unrest that the shooting spawned was even a bigger eye opener to a suburban white kid, who would end up graduating in a class that had only *two* black students out of over six hundred.

It also increased my political interest which was high anyway. My dad, who later in his life did what many do and became increasingly conservative, was a Kennedy Democrat, probably as much for the fact that he actually got to hang out at the Kennedy compound a couple of times and play touch football with the clan. So certainly it was impactful to me when President John Kennedy was killed, but I was only 7, and while sad, it did not affect me deeply.

But I really got into the presidential campaign of Bobby Kennedy, and a large part of it was how he seemed to connect with black Americans (using the terms of the time) as well as whites. Certainly there was a bit if naivety involved on my part, but in subsequent readings of history, I do feel that Bobby Kennedy truly felt that he could make an impact in racial relations, maybe affected by his brother's foot-dragging on the issue earlier in the decade.

His campaign gained momentum, and my anticipation for the summer's political conventions was palpable (I won't blame you if you chuckle). A big primary day in early June would conclude with the results of the massively important California primary. Of course Kennedy won it, and I had been allowed by my parents to stay up late to see the results. The acceptance speech to come would never occur because he was shot, and we know now that he really never had a chance to live. But when I went to bed, he was alive and when I woke up, he was still hanging on as I went to school.

I will forever be grateful for the fact that Miss Rubinwitch allowed me to leave class and go into a separate room and watch the coverage on television. She knew that I truly cared, as did she, and she allowed me a privilege maybe I shouldn't have had.

Soon it became official that Bobby Kennedy was dead. I can very honestly say that changed me very drastically as a person. I was a blissfully happy young man who had succeeded at about everything I touched, which allowed me to kind of breeze along through my early life. I was also a hopeless romantic with a sunshiny disposition.

There are probably few things that an 11-year-old boy wants to be called less than a "sweet kid." But that was me. Everybody who talks about me at that time says that same thing. But I had been injected with some serious cynicism that spring. Of course, many people think that happened to our country as well. I think some of that was for the good. It's not like the *Mad Men* lifestyle was without warts.

But the hope that people like Martin Luther King or Bobby Kennedy, or perhaps somebody else you would like to pick out, could be snuffed out so savagely, left a major mark. I have still spent most of my days as a happy person, but anybody who knows me knows that while I feel like I see mostly the good, there is an undercurrent there.

That attitude has been changed for the better this year as I have made my little journey. I tend a little more to think "good for them," when before I would think that certain hobbies or passions were trite or ignorant. I make a point to soak in the good experiences or fun moments that come along. I smile a bit more warmly at some things that maybe I chuckled snarkily about before.

To a point.

Of course, the sixth grade would end soon after that, and that meant the end of elementary school, and the end of having Miss Rubinwitch as my teacher, and really an early mentor. She moved up to junior high teaching, but at a different school. I would see her from time to time the next couple of years.

I'm not positive whether it was three or four years later, something like that, when I went to visit her at the school she was at, and the nameplate for her class said "Mrs. Friedberg." It is extremely silly, buy my heart sank. I have no idea what the hell I expected, but I'm just telling the truth.

Mr. Friedberg got a great catch, and they are still happily married. About 10 years ago through Facebook research we reconnected. We got to go to dinner a couple of times and it was really wonderful. It had been many years, but we still had a great connection. She had the sparkle in her eye and the wit and intelligence that made me admire her.

My 6th grade class. I'm in the front row, second from the right.

We email back and forth pretty often now, and at the risk of betraying her to her other students (she actually later became a college counselor), we address each other as FFT (Favorite Former Teacher), and FFS (Favorite Former Student). She probably had other students who were in the running, but I didn't. She was the best teacher I ever had by a mile, and my life has been enriched by knowing her.

My good friend John, who was a teacher, died a couple of years ago. John was a unique guy, and he was extremely crusty and cynical, but our group of friends from college that stayed close all loved the guy. But you would describe him as "difficult."

However, at his memorial service, you saw the other side of it. Students of his from his very first class to his last days as a teacher rose and spoke about how Mr. Cound made such an important impact on their lives. It was revealing and more than just a little touching. That's the impact a teacher can have on young lives when they care enough.

It sure happened to me. There is a special place on the wall of my office, where there is a painting that Mrs. Friedberg crafted a few years ago. It is a lovely seascape of a New England coastline spot, I think Cape Cod. It puts a smile on my face every time I look at it.

The last few months of my age 11 were a great sports highlight that I remember in a very odd way. I was a very good baseball player from a young age. I can thank my dad for that, and some natural aptitude. Dad started tossing a ball at my brother Jim (one year younger) and me from about the time were could stand up. He pitched to us a lot, and we loved it. Apparently, at least in part to that I could always hit, was a pretty fast runner, and could throw quite well.

When we lived in the little town of Hopkinton (the site of the start of the Boston Marathon), I was the biggest fish in the small pond of Little League Baseball, and that gave me a lot of confidence (undoubtedly too much) as well. Our family moved to Framingham when I was nine, it had about 10 times more people that Hopkinton, but I still could more than hold my own, and I was one of the few players of age 9 to play in the 12 and under league.

We convened for practice in the spring of that year. I was an outfielder going into my 11-year-old season. The first day of practice, a new kid joined the team; at least we thought it was just one new kid. The one we thought was joining our team was a very talented looking player who we learned was 10. The person with him we all thought had driven him to practice since he looked 16. He was 12 and he was also joining the team.

He was about 6-feet tall, and we already had another player about that stature, and those two alternated at pitcher and catcher. It became evident in practice games they were going to strike out about 13 batters per game out of the 18 outs. So my coach moved me to first base so that I would actually touch the ball and contribute defensively.

We rolled through our league (there were two in town), and I was the leading hitter. But hardly the leading hitter in both leagues! Second, but by a country mile. My mom kept the article previewing the "World Series" of Framingham. I can proudly read that I led the National League in hitting with my .505 average. But the next sentence provided the humbling words "Rick Crowley enters the Series leading the Colts and the American League with his .681 average!!!!!!!!!! (my exclamation points).

You'll notice throughout I am not using many people's names. If I do, it's either because it's something very positive about them, or I know them well enough to know they won't mind. If I ever write a true full memoir, it will include everything, and I will have died and handed it to someone else. Rick became a good friend of mine in high school, and at a reunion a few years ago, it was fun to tell his wife the story of how his batting average dwarfed mine.

We swept the two out of three series in two games, and I had the game winning hit in the clincher. The extremely odd thing is, I am blessed (or cursed) with a tremendous memory, and can dredge up the most minor details of things that occurred many, many years ago. But as far as that season when I was one of the best players in a big town and helped win a championship, literally about the only clear memory I have is of the line drive single up the middle that drove in the deciding run. It's a bit of a real regret, actually, and a weird quirk, but it is what it is.

Our championship year came at the end of my 11-year-old year. At the beginning in 1967 Carl Yastrzemski had captivated New England with the Boston Red Sox rags to riches story of a downtrodden team that in one year went from the outhouse to the seventh game of the World Series, only to lose for a third time to Bob Gibson, putting on a virtuoso performance. Really quite similar to the Kansas City Royals 2014 journey that happened at the time my journey through cancer and recovery began.

9.

TRAIL OF TEARS

June 3rd, 2015 - Day 6
Murdo, South Dakota to Pierre, South Dakota - just 55 miles

The day dawned on my second day of toning down the driving distance. So, the morning decision landed on the state capital of Pierre as the destination for the day. I never started any day with a complete plan, but I also never left town one place without a hotel selected in the next either.

Today's bike ride, which is a recurring theme, not only saw me cover the whole town, but I also rode my bike on every paved road in Murdo. It's the county seat, but only 475 people live here. There are, however, 11 motel properties. The apparent reason is the car show that is located here, which includes an ersatz museum. When I arrived the day before I wanted to grab an ice cream, but just ahead of me streamed in about 30 people who were together. I noticed they had strong accents and were wearing shirts that said, "Kiwi's on Route 66." They were all driving Mustangs, and as it turns out, I had been driving near them for the last 50 miles.

There was also a sign for "The Big Variety Show." I really can't even summon up a thought on how bad I imagine it might be. I didn't give it a go, and don't even know how often it runs. Perhaps I am wrong, seeing as something keeps 11 motels open.

As my bike ride was concluding, I rode past the Iversen Motel, just down the street from mine. The door was open to one of the outside entry rooms, and a man was cleaning the room. I have stayed in a million hotels and motels in my travels, and I can say with certainty that was the first time I had seen a man cleaning one. Darned if two days later I saw the same thing in Valentine, Nebraska.

As you have already been able to tell, I find small town America somewhat fascinating. But I can't imagine growing up in a town as small as this. It's many miles to anywhere else, everybody must know every little thing about you, and what the hell do you do? I might have become a better golfer or ball-player, because it does seem as if that would be the only thing to do.

Generally, each morning I just got up when I felt like it, but on this morning, I had to rise by 7:30 or so to get my bike ride in since there was no set checkout time at the old American Inn Motel. The lady informed me when I checked in the previous day that checkout was based on when the cleaning ladies decided to show up for work, which sometimes was as early as 8:30. There were only three patrons staying at the less-than-luxury digs, so I had to actually set an alarm, which wasn't part of the program.

I said it wasn't luxury, but the motel was OK, and it was a bit of a labor of love, or survival for the older lady who ran it. I had a conversation with her. She had lived for years in Murdo, but her husband had passed away a few years ago, and she moved to Oregon to be close to children and grandkids. But something called her to return to her hometown.

She started working at the motel, and when the owners

For better or worse, this *is why Murdo, South Dakota, has 11 hotels.*

retired to Florida, they gave her the property. She said that it kept her busy and energized, and you kind of got the idea that it was the thing that helped her fight off the loneliness of surviving past her husband of 44 years. She was a nice lady, but her words carried a lot of melancholy. I liked her, and my memories of her and the motel that is her lifeline will not fade.

Since I was only going to drive for about an hour or so, I decided that I would give a try to "1880s Town," a tourist attraction that I had passed about 20 miles down the road yesterday. The flashing sign next to the highway said it had been featured in *The New York Times*, and on various television shows, and was where the movie *Dances With Wolves* was filmed. Looked a bit tacky, but what the heck.

It was about a half-hour drive, and the serendipitous event

occurring on the way was the fact that on my satellite radio old-time Radio channel, which I listen to as much or more than any other, was an episode of *Gunsmoke*. I'm sure many people are familiar with the television show with James Arness, but the radio version is very well done. William Conrad is the voice of Matt Dillon.

Conrad is an interesting example of the wonderful illusion of radio dramas. He has an outstanding voice, and is all over this channel in various shows. He sounds very much the leading man, and his tough, but caring version of Matt Dillon is great. He also, of course, is a close "friend" of the local madam Miss Kitty. So the upshot is that, on the radio, William Conrad is cool. He also was a short, bald man who weighed over 300 pounds.

It is a testimony to his skills and charisma as an actor that after his outstanding radio career he made the transition to television, and may well have been the most unlikely leading man tough guy detective when he played the lead role in *Cannon*, a very successful 70s television show.

It was just plain ironic and neat that my preparation for "1880s Town" was an episode of *Gunsmoke*. It was rather a grisly chapter for the Marshall of Dodge City, but also carried a very sympathetic (for the time, 1955) message regarding Native Americans. There were a flurry of deaths of both white men and Indians as the episode concluded, and Matt Dillon concluded with a message regarding the desperation of the Indians, whose lifeline, the buffalo, was being wiped out.

I literally sat in my car in the parking lot of the attraction to hear the last five minutes of Gunsmoke, and then it was time for the gates to "1880s Town" to open.

Just outside of Murdo, this is an 1880s town that could have been so much more.

It was worth the effort. You start by going through an exhibit of many artifacts from *Dances with Wolves*, with several on-the-set pictures of Kevin Costner. There are some teepees, and the stuffed version of the actual horse that Costner rode in the movie.

The "town" itself was a bit disappointing. If I had been there maybe 10 years before, it might have been excellent. There were outstanding restorations of actual buildings of the town. The jail, a couple of residences, the general store, a hotel, etc. But they had been allowed to go into complete disrepair. Layers of dust were on everything, things had broken, and some areas were roped off because of potential danger.

I actually said to someone, "This would be really cool if they kept it up," and that person replied "Well, they want it to be authentic." Uh, *no*, there wasn't an inch of dust on someone's bed when they lived there, and there wasn't caked rust on the bottom of the tub at the best hotel in town. If you are ever traveling near Murdo, I hope that someone has invested a little cash in old "1880s Town," because it could be really quite something.

It certainly only would take a little industry, because they *have* done that with one building ... the saloon. It is shiny and clean, you can buy snacks, and sasparilla, rent western costumes to wear around town, and there is a piano player entertaining, and a couple of saloon girls parading around. But you can risk getting ill from the dust and mold in the other buildings.

It was only about an hour to Pierre, and I was a little invigorated to not have a long drive today. Golf was perhaps going to be on the agenda. I arrived at my motel about 2 o'clock. It was a nice, family run spot, and the people at the front desk were friendly. They asked me about the purpose of my travels, and of course, there really wasn't one, but they got part of the story.

The young man who was working the front desk with his mom clearly seemed to pick up on the vagabond nature of this endeavor because he suggested that I might like to go the circus, which was in town. I suppose he might have been thinking that I might want to *join* the circus. I actually gave some thought to going, not joining, but opted for some golf instead.

It was a nice, municipal course, not too busy, and it was a beautiful afternoon. I played by myself, which I actually often do, and very much enjoyed the afternoon, despite a lackluster 83 that could have been much better. I concluded the round and sat on the deck having a beer. I texted my wife, as per the daily plan, that I was safe, and that I was in Pierre, South Dakota. I had kept to my plan of not speaking with anyone, but her usual loving return text included the thought that she was wearying of not hearing my voice. That was nice to hear.

So I decided to give her a short call, the only one I would make the entire time. It was a little weird making the call. She is the best wife you could have, and her understanding of my whim, while expected, was touching. It was almost like calling for a first date. She was having dinner with a friend, and sounded surprised to hear my voice. I said a few things, but could not stay on long because it's difficult to speak when you are crying, even if it's a real happy cry ... which it was.

•   •   •   •   •

I tend to be a little more reflective these days after what has transpired the past year, although I actually have always kind of been that way. I remember once when I was 12, I was over at the schoolyard near our home. I was by myself and was riding on the swing set and stuff like that late in the afternoon. It was getting to be about 5 o'clock, and I had a little league game at six. After the previous year's championship season, it was kind of just a decent year for the Phillies. I was the best remaining player on the squad, which basically always meant that you pitched. I wasn't a great pitcher, and I didn't much like it either. So for half the games, it wasn't that much fun for me.

I still liked playing, but on this day, I was laying around in the sun daydreaming, and the thought crossed my mind that I would rather do this than play ball that night. I don't know if you would say I didn't have the courage to make that unorthodox choice, or just that I did the right thing, but I eventually scrambled home in time to make the game ... but not by much.

•　•　•　•　•

When I finished up my emotional call to my wife, it was still early evening, and I decided to drive around and see if it looked as if there was anything fun to do. It was a little late for the last circus show of the day, but maybe I should have done that. I always checked the local paper and other media like that for potential things to do in these small burgs, but there was wasn't much to offer in the old *Capital-Journal,* Pierre's local paper, as far as events.

I drove up past the state capitol, and a short distance away there was a nice ball field where the lights were just starting to take effect. There was an American Legion game being played and you could park on the side of the street and have a good view of the field. There was a pretty good gathering of fans on a beautiful late spring night with the sun setting watching the teenagers play ball.

It was an easy decision to hang out and watch a couple of innings. It was baseball in the purest form and it was a delight. It took me back to playing, but since it was American Legion ball, it even took me back to my first professional radio job.

I had done a lot of stuff in radio growing up, and interspersed in my college years, I worked professionally at a few stations, but my first full-time radio job after college was at WMRC in Milford, Massachusetts. It was a very typical small town station, with a familiar at-the-time format of some music, news, sports, and local sports events.

It's a bit different from small town radio that you might

have experienced in the Midwest or other more spread out areas with smaller populations. In some of those places, the only way to access AM radio might be that small town station. Conversely, as in most places in the Northeast, population density is great, and large communities abound. Milford was a small town, but it's only about 30 miles from Boston, and about 20 from Worcester, a city of about 200,000 people.

So if you lived in Milford, you could listen to all the large stations in those cities. That meant you had to really want to listen to WMRC. Many days that meant you really had to want to listen to me. I had a disc jockey shift from 9 a.m. to 1 p.m. I was the afternoon newsman, I had a sports talk show from 6 - 7 p.m., and I did all the play-by-play of the games that we did.

One of the teams was the local American Legion team. Milford had about 20,000 people living there then, but they would routinely have upward of 2,000 people at times at their home games. So many folks in town were very interested in the games. We did them all, but the big sell was the road games, since many of the fans were older and while they enjoyed getting out their lawn chairs and such and going to the game in Milford, they didn't usually drive the 20 miles or so to the various other towns that Milford played at.

That is except when we had some technical issue, which wasn't all that uncommon. Our little remote broadcast unit needed only a phone line to operate, but that was often dicey. We would order the lines, and they were supposed to be strung so that they would be available at the backstop, and I usually set up behind the screen at home plate. But it wasn't unusual at all to show up and find that the promised line wasn't there. It was 1984 at this point and obviously there were no cell phones, so every half-hour or so I would find a pay phone and call in a report on how the game was going. But the dedicated fans wouldn't get full play-by-play.

This would create a remarkable site. The fans were used to occasionally not getting their promised game, and when the announcement came over the air that due to technical difficulties they would only get the phone reports, they would pile into their cars and hit the road.

About a half-hour after the announcement, a line of cars would start to come into the parking lot of the road ballpark. Sometimes they would number over a hundred, and they were never happy with me. I had always exhausted all possibilities. I once ran about three hundred feet of cord from a bar, but sometimes no go.

But I was the only one that they could complain to, and I got an earful many times from a very annoyed senior citizen who no doubt had settled down on the couch after a nice dinner ready to listen to some baseball. I had ruined that, and I took the heat.

During my coverage of the 2015 American League Championship Series between the Royals and the Blue Jays, I struck up a conversation with the Jays first basemen Chris Colabello. I had noticed on his bio that he was born in Framingham, Massachusetts, my hometown. It turns out he was only born in Framingham because the hospital was there—he was actually from Milford.

Around 15 years after I broadcast those games, he had played for the same American Legion team, and we exchanged some stories about the ultra enthusiastic fans that supported the team. I noticed that he had no Boston accent whatsoever, and asked him about that. He replied, "I hate that (bleeping) accent, I purposely got rid of it when I was eight. When I go back and see my old friends I still give them (grief) about theirs."

I don't know if the American Legion fans here in Pierre were quite as dedicated as Milford's, but a very respectable amount of them had gathered on this lovely night in early June. It was a very American scene, and it fit in very nicely. When it grew dark and I had watched the game for about an hour, it was time to go.

· · · · ·

I was packing in quite a lot each day, and that meant that I was usually pretty cashed in by the middle of the evening. I went back to the motel, used the indoor pool and Jacuzzi, and that really did it. Another night where the time between me resting my head on the pillow and falling asleep probably didn't reach five minutes.

10.

NAKED ICONS

June 4, 2015 - Day Seven
Pierre, South Dakota to Valentine, Nebraska - 131 miles

I have generally had such wonderful weather on this trip, and when there has been some inclemency, it has been timed nicely. I woke up this morning in the second smallest state capital by population in the country, Pierre, South Dakota; I would bet that it is also the most often mispronounced capital (it is pronounced PEER). Only Montpelier, Vermont, is less populous than the 13,000 or so that live here. Looking at the radar on my computer, I could see a wide band of showers bearing down on us, so I scrambled quickly to get the bike out for the daily tour of a town.

It was one of the best rides of the trip, and they were all quite good. Being the state capital obviously means quite a few good jobs for the townspeople, and it showed. The area around the state capital building and surrounding state offices was beautiful. The capital area is on a bluff probably 500 feet or so above the main downtown area. Large mature trees, and small lakes and ponds made a lovely setting for nice old homes built on wide boulevards that really could have managed four lanes, but featured only two.

A striking state capitol building in Pierre, South Dakota, the second smallest capital city in the United States.

Riding around the town, you got the feeling that at least half of the town's population was employed in some fashion related to the town's standing as the state capital. Many I'm sure work for the various agencies that have their offices named for famous South Dakotans.

The Department of Environment and Natural Resources building is named for Joe Foss. If you are around my age and don't recognize the name, you weren't paying much attention, well, at least to things that I was. Among a myriad of accomplishments that included World War II fighter pilot ace, governor of South Dakota, and a whole lot more, Foss was also the first commissioner of the American Football League.

He was obviously a good commissioner as the league grew from nothing to prominence in the six years he was there. Of course, the league featured very powerful owners, so it's hard to know if ole' Joe was the driving force behind all of that. After he stepped down, for seven years he was the host of "The American Sportsman" on ABC, one of the most successful shows of its kind ever on television. It's a reflection of how much we had to watch in those days of basically three channels that I watched that show as a kid all the time, and I have never hunted, and fished only a handful of times in my life.

The famous broadcaster Curt Gowdy often was featured on the show, and I have lots of familiarity with the Hall of Fame broadcaster. Before he became the leading TV sportscaster in the country for about a decade, he worked in Boston, doing the Red Sox and many other things. As we have noted before, my father was in those circles then, and as a young kid, I had many great experiences and opportunities related to games and broadcasts.

But the only time I actually met Curt Gowdy, he was naked … pause… pause …

My dad had taken me and my brother Jim to a Boston Patriots game at Fenway Park. The Patriots somewhat reflected the early vagabond nature of the AFL. The Pats played everywhere, Fenway, Harvard Stadium, Boston University Field (the old home of baseball's Boston Braves), and Boston College's Alumni Stadium. After the game at Fenway, we had the chance to go into the Patriots locker room.

Gowdy had done the game on TV and must have had somewhere important to go, since he was availing himself of the team's showers. I was seven and my brother was six, standing there with my dad awe-struck at the site of these gigantic behemoth football players strolling about undressed after the game.

My dad knew Gowdy, and when he came out of the showers,

my father (who is no shrinking violet) bellowed at him to come over and meet his boys. Over came the iconic broadcaster, and he politely greeted us and shook our hands ... with no clothes on.

Alrighty then.

We subsequently met Jim Nance (not Nantz, the broadcaster, but the All-AFL running back). He was a huge barrel of a man, and the first African-American person I had met personally. He was as nice as he was gigantic, and he had also just departed the shower. You don't really forget something like that, but I'd like to thank my bike ride past the Joe Foss building in Pierre, South Dakota, for jogging the memory.

● ● ● ● ●

It was another shortish drive today, a bit over two hours south down Route 63 to Valentine, Nebraska. I had made a phone call just before I left and actually *spoke* to a person, and the favor I received would create one of the many highlights of the journey.

This excursion began with the great hospitality of Randy Towner at Firekeeper Golf Course in Mayetta, Kansas. After all the wonderful scenery and small town events, people and experiences, it was time for a golf highlight. With Randy's help, I was about have one of the greatest golf experiences of my life.

The day that I was at Firekeeper, I had asked Randy if he had any connections at the renowned Sand Hills golf courses. There are a Nicklaus and a Tom Doak course there, and it's famous for the quality of the courses, but also the remote location in Mullen, Nebraska, which is reached by a single lane dirt road. There is an airstrip there, however, to allow the more well heeled to fly in for a golf getaway.

Randy said he did not, but he talked to his superintendant, and told me that if my trip took me toward Valentine, Nebraska, to give him a call. So I did, and he said he would see if there was a hookup at The Prairie Club, outside Valentine, since the going rate was too steep for me. Free certainly wasn't, and thanks to Randy that would be my green fee at this course. I had no idea what to expect, but I was excited.

I settled in to another fairly spartan, but pleasant, motel in Valentine, Nebraska. It was called the Raine Motel, and the pretty young lady at the check-in shrugged off the fact that I had an online reservation print out, but she didn't have one on her computer. As it turned out, this saved me 10 bucks, since their daily rate was less than the online one. Life's little victories.

It was a cloudy, warmish day with medium winds, which would prove to be absolutely perfect. It was midafternoon when I headed out of Valentine, which is pretty remote in itself with a population, under four thousand, and south on Route 20 out into the country toward The Prairie Club. It was definite Sand Hills terrain, although it is 90 miles northeast of the Sand Hills golf courses.

About 20 miles out there is the smallest of signs indicating the club, and you turn onto a sandy, unpaved road. Around 3 miles of winding road and you start to spy some golf holes, and I knew I was in for a treat. Carved into the rolling landscape were two golf courses. There was a very nice, huge clubhouse, a few cabins ... and that's it.

Out here in the middle of nowhere, I was going to play The Dunes Course. The other one is The Pines. It was late afternoon when I teed off, and it was a long drive in the cart to the first tee. Right away, it was evident that it would be special. The

Sand Hills links land is perfect for golf courses, in fact when I first had started driving out of Broken Bow a few days ago in my first pass through the Sand Hills, I kept thinking, man, you could put a golf course here ... and here ... and here.

After a few holes on this slightly breezy, cloudy day with no one in sight, I had the distinct feeling that I was playing golf in Scotland, which I have never done. And if I never do, I will certainly have had a wonderfully reasonable facsimile. The architects had all the land that they wanted, and they used it. It also became evident quickly that you had the tremendous experience of playing each golf hole, and not being able to even see another hole. Since I was playing by myself, this created a spectacular solitude.

It's funny about playing golf, though. The first few holes I was just soaking in the experience, literally almost transported to another part of the world in my mind, openly speaking out loud about how cool this was. But then I was making the turn and started to realize that things were going well. I was only a couple of shots over par, and this was a very hard course. So then starting the back nine I went bogey, double bogey, bogey, double bogey. I was furious, and was calling myself things I would never call my worst enemy.

I got to the next tee box and gave myself a little talking to. "Hey, idiot, this is about as cool an experience as you could possibly have, let's not jack it up because you are not going to shoot a fancy score." I looked around at the vistas which were as enjoyable for a fan of links golf courses as you could have, and got a smile back on my face. I played OK the last few holes, but that was far from the point. I got to soak in something special.

There in one more note for the more golf oriented of you.

It took about seven holes for me to realize that what I thought would be an impossible course to walk was actually a brilliant design for that. In my cart playing the fourth tees from the back (still 6,500 yards), the drives from the previous green to the next tee box seemed extremely long. But I eventually realized that if you were walking and playing the back tees, the next tee was no more than one hundred yards from the previous green.

For a golfer, it was an almost mystical experience. The solitude of the afternoon was completely fitting for this journey. I saw only one other group of golfers, at a remarkable distance away. The wind was blowing on my face, which was (mostly) stuck in a wonderful grin. It was incredible.

This was another place, where at least on a Thursday night, the motel bar seemed to be about the only place people went, and in fact on this night, not many people even went there. The NBA finals were being played and I watched some of that in my room while I cleaned up. Hoping for a little civilization, I took the lengthy, 50-step walk to the bar.

It ended up being a great way to finish off a golf-oriented day. The assistant pro from the Prairie Club was one of the few people there, and we ended up having a wonderful conversation ... well at least for a couple of guys who love golf. We talked about architecture, and what we liked and didn't about certain golf courses and types of golf courses. It was perfect.

Golf has been a wonderful lifelong companion. Which is kind of odd, since I didn't play golf at all until I was 11, played through high school, didn't play that much in my twenties, but from that point forward it has been more than a passion.

I obviously had some aptitude for it, since the first time I played was basically the last time I didn't break 50 for nine holes. After a stereotypical end to what probably could have been a pretty decent run as a baseball player, I say stereotypically, since just about every weekend warrior has a tale of some bad break or bad coach, who screwed him. I won't bore you with mine, but the result of it is that I switched to high school golf as a sophomore.

I actually was pretty good despite zero instruction, and the fact that since my mom didn't drive, I missed golf practice often. The Framingham Country Club was about 10 miles from my house. I still was the top player on the team, and did get to play in the state golf championships at The Country Club in Brookline, Massachusetts.

The Country Club was the site of the 1988 U.S. Open, the first of the back-to-back wins by Curtis Strange. I covered the event for my radio station in Utica, New York. I was starting to play a lot of golf at that point, and was a ridiculously dedicated fan of the sport. I pretty much knew every golfer down through the Asian Tour. I still am pretty good about that, but not quite to the insane level.

That's not the story, though. I had broken up with my live-in girlfriend a few months before, and pretty much been left with nothing of substance, except the apartment. She wasn't real happy about the whole deal and I think I had a bed, a TV, a couple of pots and pans, and a fork. No car either.

So I went to an advertiser on our station to get something to drive. I was making about 18 thousand a year, and had no savings. So I asked the man to get me the cheapest new car that he could summon up with the lowest payment, and with no down payment. The result, I was the proud owner of a sparkling blue 1988 Yugo. That's right, baby.

I actually kind of liked the car. It was mine at the very least. I'll give you an idea of the quality of the fine Yugoslavian vehicle. On the drive from upstate New York to Brookline, Massachusetts, for the Open, there are a lot of rolling hills. I could go the speed limit of 55 going uphill ... with the pedal slammed to the floorboard.

The first day at the Open, I went through the gates with my credentials to the media parking, which had about three different checkpoints. At each one I got a pretty cool reception to say the least. To say The Country Club is a stuffy place is the wildest of understatements. The primary color of the place is light yellow, the buildings are yellow, the blazers on the well-heeled volunteers are yellow, and the ladies generally were wearing yellow summer dresses as they sashayed around the premises of a club I ordinarily would have needed a gun to get into.

With my full credential I pretty much had the run of the place. I certainly drew a lot of sideways glances with my shoulder length hair and beard. I didn't much care. I was in a very carefree time of my life, and this summer was basically one giant smile after another. After my treatment the first day, each of the succeeding days I entered the premises with the windows of my Yugo down, and AC/DC blaring at full volume. I just held my credential out the window and cruised on in.

Don't have any ill thoughts about the young lady who wasn't very happy when I broke up with her and took all the furniture and car. She would become my first wife and the mother of my two lovely daughters.

Tracy was also my wife when I had the luxury of playing the most golf of my life, and play it in a reasonably competitive environment. I was doing morning drive in Utica, New York, in the early 1900s. Our children had not been born yet. I had to be at work at 4 a.m. and work on the AM and FM stations in a very busy schedule. But I usually could get out of the office by noon.

I was by this point extremely dedicated to my running and was in the relatively early stages of my almost 20-year streak. Because I wanted to get out to the golf course after work, I would ordinarily rise at about 2:30 in the morning to run, get a shower, and get off to work.

There was a beautiful golf course about 15 miles out of town, The Golf Club of Newport. It was an old course that had fallen into disrepair until it was purchased and rescued by a man named Pete Grygiel, who was the owner and superintendant. It was a labor of love, and a family business. Because the course had been in such bad shape, and the perception was that it was a lot further away than it was, it was not heavily played.

My wife worked regular hours, and as I said we had no children. We would meet at the gym about 5:30. So I had all afternoon to play. I walked the lovely, hilly, tree lined golf course for 27 holes every single weekday. Anybody's golf game would benefit under these circumstances, and I had some natural talent, and I was playing the same golf course over and over. My handicap dropped to as low as 3.4, and would have been lower if I had been any good at all under pressure.

I played a lot of the local tournaments, and even played a couple of U.S. Mid Amateur qualifiers. I learned much to my dismay how different it is to play regular golf and tournament golf. I never played "as well as I could" in these events. I wasn't alone, but I was probably one of the worst offenders. Before one year's club championship, four of us who were considered among the favorites played 36 holes for decent stakes to prep for the event. I shot 73 and 74 and beat them.

Then came the tournament. My 147 would have won, but I didn't approach it. I shot 81-82 and wasn't much of a factor. The other guys didn't play as well either, but nothing like me. Mr.Grygiel was a big supporter of me. He saw how dedicated I was to practicing and playing, and expressed surprise that I hadn't done better. He shouldn't have been. I would see it unfold more than a couple of times.

The failures didn't diminish my love of the game, even though I beat myself up something awful on the golf course. I am an extremely relaxed and easygoing person, probably to a fault, in every area of my life. With the large exception of competition. From pickup basketball, to softball, to golf, to … well, everything where you keep score, I am really wildly competitive. I think that it perhaps stems from the fact that when I was a young athlete, and was better than most, I took it for granted and didn't exhibit this ruthless competitive streak.

Maybe I had a great combination for trying to get through a trying time like the cancer and the treatment. The stubborn competitiveness and the somewhat matter-of-fact side to just take what comes along maybe is a good one for something like this. More likely, it's just good treatment, and good fortune.

Thursday was waning and Friday was beckoning. It had been another long and full and wonderful day. It wasn't just Friday that was beckoning. Home was beginning to. I'm not the type to get homesick because I always know that I will be back there soon, but I also knew I was going to be ready. As with every night on the journey, it wasn't more than a minute or three from head hitting the pillow to dead asleep.

11.

AGE 26
FACTORY BLUES AND
SHEEPSKIN REDEMPTION

I'm not sure it much matters, but this chapter isn't really about age 26 per se, although it is a good finishing point. It's more about the years leading up to the culmination of an extremely tumultuous time in my life. The age 26 part was actually a whole lot of fun, among other things, it was when I finally graduated from college. You see, I didn't take the typical four-year route.

I've seen the movie; I know the joke about someone being in school that long is for doctors. But I actually wasn't in college for all that time. I graduated from college in about five and a half years, which isn't speedy but it's not what you might have been thinking.

At the University of Kansas, my determination to finish where I started led to a rather amazing string of tough times, funny stories, heartbreak, and eventually, incredible personal satisfaction.

After high school, having never left New England in my life, I got on a train in Boston, and headed west as America was getting past Watergate and Nixon and Vietnam, and seemingly trying to settle into "normalcy" after an important and turbulent decade. I selected KU from a group of five state schools. I had to

go to a state school for monetary reasons. As my dad wa:
ing for what would be his best ever television job, the station
he was slated to work for was in the middle of a licensing battle
which would go all the way to the Supreme Court. So finances
were tight at that time.

I wanted to go away to school anyway, and find a large
state university that played major conference sports, because
I wanted the training of broadcasting those games. The group
of schools I applied to was Georgia, Iowa, Idaho, Washington
State, and Kansas. The dichotomy of my high school academics
is reflected in the school responses. Washington State wouldn't
have me because I hadn't graduated in the upper half of my
class, and Georgia wanted me in their Advanced Placement program because my test scores were so high. I had basically made
A's in high school if I cared for the class, or barely passed or
worse if I didn't.

Both of these schools were out, Georgia because I wasn't
much interested in working as hard as Advanced Placement
would have required. In addition to the lack of desire for an
academic grind, I had a close friend who was a highly recruited
tennis player, and he said I wouldn't like Georgia. Iowa was
always kind of a long shot.

Now all this decision-making was basically done by study-
ing brochures, so I'm hardly going to call it scientific. They were
all good journalism schools. KU was, for some reason always
the front-runner, although I think if Idaho had been playing in a
major conference I might have gone there.

So KU it was, and after four years, I wasn't done (that's
another book). My parents had footed the bill, and even though
it was microscopic by today's standard, I made the decision

to find a way to finish on my own. Well, sort of. I went home for a couple of years and worked. I was doing some part time radio work along with other jobs just to make money, and I was doing some games and such, so I probably didn't even have to finish college to start a career in radio.

But I was determined to do so, and I was determined to do it at KU. So after that time at home, I headed back out to Kansas without much savings, hoping to work for a year or so and make enough money to complete the full year of credits I needed. It took three years to get to that point, three of the craziest years you could ever experience.

When I arrived back I had a little money and got a decent apartment, but it was harder than I thought in that recessional time to find decent work. Although it was a bad time to try and make a few thousand dollars, I can't say that was the only reason that things deteriorated to the point that I hit the nadir in an $80 a month room in a house that rented to nine different people.

That room was about the only thing separating me from homelessness at that time. I was basically broke. I had quit a job I hated because of an ogre shift supervisor at Burger King. He was actually the father of the manager, and a very bitter man who was not happy that circumstances had him working under his son at a fast food operation.

He constantly dogged all of us on the most trivial of matters, and I in particular was consistently at odds with him. It only took a week for this to come to a head. He told me never to speak to the girls up front, but the only communication we really ever had was to confirm orders. He persisted in this, and finally I threw my stylish paper hat at him and walked out. The manager knew his dad was difficult and he tried to get me to return, but when he said I would have to continue to work on his dad's shifts I couldn't. Honor over paycheck, stupidity over practicality.

Especially dumb because it was hard to get another job when you didn't even have a phone. I would walk around Lawrence all day, fill out job applications, and used the phone number of a friend when asked where I could be reached. Basically, if I wasn't hired on the spot, it wasn't going to happen.

But another friend of mine had been working at the Stokely-Van Camp bean factory in East Lawrence, and he told me they were coming out of a layoff period and would be hiring quite a few people. The process was, you walked in, did the most basic of interviews, and if you could breathe you got a job. The pay was very good for the type of work.

So why you might ask, was it so easy to get *that* job? Because anyone who knew anything about the place, knew just how miserable a job it was. The only saving grace is that you had a *variety* of awful tasks, the pay was good, and overtime was plentiful.

The first day I worked would be the first time that I ever went running. I loved playing sports, but just running? That seemed crazy to me. I literally was astounded in high school that guys would run all three sports seasons. Cross country, indoor track, and outdoor track. Doing something like that was the furthest thing from my mind.

But it was blistering hot that first day at the bean factory. It was well over a hundred degrees outside, which meant it was about 150 degrees inside the plant as the beans were steamed and cooked in gigantic tanks at very high temperatures.

I don't remember which of the miserable tasks I did that first day, but all I know is that when I walked out the door of the plant about 6 o'clock, 108 degrees felt like about 75 and pleasant. I had walked the 3 miles to work from my fleabag room to the plant, and when I came out to go home, I just started running, basically Forest Gump-like. I didn't make it the whole way that first day, but soon I would and actually would extend the route. My running streak didn't start until a few years later, but I can tell you for sure, I ran home basically every day that I worked there.

Just for context, this miserable work in the end was a very powerful impetus in my life. My work ethic in everything I did improved drastically, because the memory of doing something you really hate just to make money to achieve a goal is an amazing motivator.

All of the tasks were pretty awful; there were just degrees of misery. There was removing the just-cooked tin cans of beans from the giant metal baskets that had come through the "cooling tanks" and moving them onto a rickety conveyer. Cooling is a relative term. When you did the regular sized cans, it wasn't so bad, since your gloves protected your hands from the searing heat.

But when we had a day where they were doing the giant gallon cans that you would get today at Costco, or a restaurant would use, that was pure hell. First off, bare hands worked far better in lifting the cans out, you could barely get anything done with the gloves on. This resulted in two joys. The first, basically burning your hands each time you picked up two at a time, and the fairly regular occurrence of cans pinching your fingers from the belt behind you, between two 10-pound containers.

Lovely.

The plant would be shut down shortly after I graduated, and with good reason. It was dirty, it was hot, and you got hurt a lot. It was so hot that you dressed in almost nothing. The smallest shorts you could get away with and a cutoff T-shirt was the uniform most of us favored. Believe it or not, women worked at this place, too. In a nice example of breaking equal rights, the ladies actually got easier jobs, like sorting out the bad beans, or running the labeling machine. The guys had no problem with that.

The grease, grime, and sweat resulted in the fact that each night when I arrived home, I took a shower and cleaned myself with a steel wool Brillo soap pad. It was an onerous process to get clean, and looking on the bright side, you had a nice and tingly feeling when you were finished, but your skin was basically scraped raw daily.

It was also pretty dangerous work, not life threatening mind you, but people got injured regularly and had to go to the emergency room. This despite the fact the place had two full-time nurses for the lesser injuries. I actually won a "safe worker" award after my first year at the plant. The only requirement to win this "coveted prize" was to *not* have gone to the hospital that year. I received a certificate that looked like a kindergarten graduation award, and a pen. I left the two of them in the break room, and my foreman Bill, thinking I forgot them, brought then to me. I not so politely told him what he could do with the items.

Less than a week later, I was hit on the head with a three hundred pound steel cage that contained a load of bean cans and was knocked cold. My cheap, little blue helmet had failed and I was sent to the hospital—my safe worker award days were over.

The worst job at the plant only came up once a month, and only when you worked Saturday overtime. Each Friday a foreman would come around with a clipboard and ask who would like to work the five hour Saturday shift. Every single time I said no, but then after thinking about it for a little while, the lure of the double time and a half it would pay was too great, and I would always change my mind.

They pretty much had to pay that rate, since the worst jobs in a place where they were almost all bad were reserved for the overtime shift. There was a clear winner in my mind for the very worst. When the cans went through the conveyer and sorter, a small percentage would be damaged and leak. The cases of beans with at least one damaged, leaking can were set aside in the warehouse, which remember was generally steaming hot.

Your task when you got this detail on Saturday went like this: You tore open the cases to sort through and pick out the offending cans. These violators had been in the warehouse for upward of a month, and usually you ripped the top of the box open to be greeted with thousands of maggots. You then gagged your way through cleaning the good cans and tossing out the bad ones. Gross is an incredible understatement. I wish I had a better term. Was double time and a half enough?

Likely the easiest job was night watchman. Whoever did this merely had to sit on their ass in the security office, and a few times overnight go check the gates. If you've seen the movie *Money Ball*, about the Oakland A's and their use of

You've gotta be cool to work in a hot factory.

Sabermetrics, you will know the answer to who the most famous alumni of the Stokely-Van Camp factory is. A photo of the plant is shown during the movie because the father of Sabermetrics, Bill James, was the night watchman. I did work the overnight shift there for a while, and we probably crossed paths, but that wouldn't have much mattered then. I would imagine he got a lot of statistical work done on that shift.

One last bean factory tale from Stokely-Van Camp. Really, the only saving grace of working at the plant was that the work seldom was nonstop. The plant was so run down and decrepit that things were constantly breaking down. On the rare days when everything went smoothly and your nine to 11 or more hour shift was nonstop work, you absolutely felt like quitting.

But this rarely happened. Right out of a scene from a movie was the best example of reprieve. If there were thunderstorms around, there was the real possibility of a power outage at the plant. If this occurred, and the outage lasted more than eight seconds, the cooking beans would be ruined, and production would cease for the shift. It would play out like this. The power went out, lights would go out, and the couple of hundred workers would start to chant a countdown in unison.

"Eight! ... Seven! ... Six! ... Five! ... Four! ... Three! ... Two! ... One! ... ZERO!!!! Total hysteria and joy would ensue. We were done for the day, released from prison, not caring about the lost hours or wages.

We got laid off in the summer of 1982. The timing for me was delicious. I had saved a pretty good chunk of money, and with one little check mark, which I now freely admit took advantage of the state, I could return to school and live pretty well. The check mark? Back then, when you filed for unemployment, all you did was fill out a card weekly with general info. But there was a box asking whether you were attending school full-time. If you checked no, you could get unemployment. Take a guess.

So my goal of graduating from KU was now realistically just two semesters away. Thank goodness I went through the torture of factory work, because it steeled my resolve for a pretty momentous challenge. I needed 40 hours of credit to graduate, and because of a couple of ill-fated prior attempts to get some course work done, which were submarined by finance, I had incompletes that had morphed into F's.

I would need to make about a 3.8 GPA for those 40 hours to boost my overall grades to the level necessary for graduation, and I intended to work extensively at the radio station as well. I also was quite adept at having a good time at that period in my life, and you can let your imagination run on that one. So I treated the schoolwork like a job. I got up every day about 6:30, got to campus before 8 o'clock, and stayed there until about 6 p. m. When I wasn't in class or on the radio, I studied and did homework.

But at 6 o'clock I was done, it was time to have fun for a few hours. Regardless of how early I would have to get up to prepare for my academics made no difference—I wanted to have a good time. Working at the plant had that kind of effect on you. You worked your butt off, and then you wanted some kind of payback. I have total and complete respect for people who toil at jobs they hate for many hours, and then return home and try to give their families normalcy. I would not be good at that.

But the course work was not a hated job or a task I dreaded. I was thrilled, full of fire for the task at hand, and the goal. I had many advantages in ripping through the course work. What I had just put myself through, with plenty of sweat equity and worse, made this seem like a cakewalk.

Also, being a 26-year-old student is an absolute blast. First off, while I'm sure many of my fellow students had a good idea I wasn't a regular college kid, they also didn't know I was *that* old. I was just another student who knew a whole lot more than most of them. The whole experience was great. I didn't much care about fitting in. I had very, very long hair and wore Indiana Jones hats, and stuff that I liked, even if somebody else might not.

One example of the fun to be had was that my completely different look and attitude was a perfect way for sorority girls to make either their boyfriends or their parents angry. I went to four different sorority formals that year after being asked to be the date for the evening. I'd like to think it was my charm and good looks, but I knew the score. I was merely a longhaired prop, but I didn't care. Beyond that, to protect the innocent, and the not so innocent, I'll just let you imagine what it was like.

As far as radio training, I had gobs of experience in broadcasting already, so getting many of the plum assignments at the student radio station wasn't much of a stretch. There was a lot of fun competition as there were many very talented broadcasters there, many of whom people in Kansas City and throughout the nation still see and hear.

I was the main (though not exclusive) play-by-play announcer for KU basketball that year on KJHK, the student station. We did the home games and a few close road games. It was the last bad season that Kansas had in college basketball. Ted Owens had done a good job there as coach, but his last couple of seasons went sideways, and 1982-83 provided many of the "last time KU did this or that" on the negative side.

People can, and do get spoiled, and starting with Larry Brown, who arrived the following season, Jayhawk fans have been spoiled ever since. But as I broadcast games in a half empty Allen Field House, I saw KU lose home games to Colorado and Nebraska, among *six* home losses. I saw losing Kansas basketball. Once I was officially out the door of the university, there would be no more losing basketball to this day.

I can't say enough about the broadcasting experience of that year. As I said before, I probably could have carved out a career without returning to college. Before returning to Lawrence I had already done the things all struggling young broadcasters do, high school games, news, 18-hour shifts, all that stuff.

But truly putting some finishing touches on not only my college degree, getting even more experience to bring to the table when I would be really trying to carve out a career, and not just do it on a part-time basis, was invaluable. Having some different voices make suggestions, and to do all this in a difficult context where I had so much on my plate, was invaluable.

The hard work really paid off. I enjoyed the grind, and made great grades, which I had to do. One of my prized moments was in Communications Law. I started the course a couple of times in other failed attempts to return to school, so I had a little edge. Other students would come to me for help with what was a very difficult course. That included some group tutorials at yet another sorority.

Sweet.

By the time the final paper was to be graded and returned, I was ahead of the game. At the start of the class the professor handed back the graded papers and saved mine for last. He then announced that I made a 98 on the research effort, and had piled up enough grade points that I didn't even have to take the final. He told me I could leave. It was a pretty big class, so it was a whole lot of fun when my fellow students treated me to a standing ovation as I departed.

The inspiration (or desperation) of the factory work fueled me to a 3.8 GPA for 40 hours of course work in two semesters. It lifted me above the required journalism school standard for graduation. I had completed the task.

I had a lot of people who were on my side, among them my roommate and subsequently lifelong friend Brien, who had offered me a place to live that got me out of the flophouse, and my girlfriend Tracy, who would later become my first wife. We were together for much of the time after my return to Lawrence, but we had some periods apart, which you could probably guess having read the chapter. But mostly it was a solitary enterprise.

They both were integral parts of one of the diversions that made a lot of the bad times leading up to achieving my goal bearable. "Rude People." That was the name of the softball team that we had in Lawrence, Kansas, for a few years. We were very good, and we lived up to the name that was inspired by the *Real People* TV show that was popular at the time. They used to give away plain T-shirts for regular events in life. Our uniform was a replica, and we played a loud, aggressive, hard running brand of game.

We had fast guys all over the place, and could run and catch everything, which was mandatory because we had no power. There was plenty of hot dog in our repertoire, and I have to confess that as the leadoff hitter, I was probably the prime offender. We had our own large group of loud fans, too. All in all, it's a good thing we won a lot because we at least could back up all of the bluster. We were deservedly a squad that everyone wanted badly to beat.

Thankfully, they had a hard time doing it, and we won a couple of Class B city championships. There were four classes of play, basically decided by quality, but decided by each team's own ambition. The reason we stayed at Class B would be confirmed at the end of each title season when they played the all city championships, and we got our comeuppance.

I mentioned our style of play did not include home runs. Well, for the champions of Class A it sure did. Each year we dispatched the Class C champ in the semifinals, while A would crunch C. Then the familiar dose of "shut your mouth" went something like this. We would do our thing and put seven or eight runs up, and catch all the balls in play. But you can't play outfield beyond the fence, and whichever Class A champ it was would hit six or seven homers, the difference in around a 15-8 loss. Still it was wonderful fun, and something to look forward to during the long factory days.

As the long awaited graduation day approached, I got a moment that everyone who has ever had a bad job or a day boss could envy. I received a call from Bill, the foreman at Stokely-Van Camp. Bill was a lifer at the plant, and he used his small amount of authority without much dignity. He *really* didn't like those of us he knew weren't going to be around long, who were going back to college. One of the guys at the plant I admired the most of ours was a co-worker who was going to KU and working there at the same time. *No way.*

The timing of Bill's call was a delight. I had one week of school left and then I was done and gone. He enthusiastically informed me that production was resuming after the months-long layoff, and said, "Time to get back to work." The call would last three more words as I replied, "Fuck you, Bill."

Not very nice at all … extremely satisfying.

Graduation day was very special with several members of my family making the long trip out. But 1,500 miles seemed like a few feet compared to the long trip to my sheepskin. Walking down the Campanile Hill at KU into the football stadium for the ceremony was one of the more emotional things I have ever done. Just like the journey in the late spring of 2015.

12.

FILM NOIR MOTEL IN A DEAD END TOWN

June 5 - Day 8
Valentine, Nebraska to Hastings, Nebraska … 233 miles

Rise and shine this morning in Valentine, after yesterday's golf-themed day, from the planning, to the great round, to the evening conversation. The bed at the Raine Motel may have been the most comfortable on the whole trip. It just shows you how little details can make a big difference.

The motel was fine, but kind of an older property and the room was quite small. Everything was decent, but the bed was extremely nice and had a plush comforter-throw pillow combination that raised the aesthetic value of the room about one thousand percent.

After the restful sleep, I got up looking forward, as usual, to my bike ride. It was a cloudy, coolish morning as I took off for another complete tour of a small town. Valentine is dead flat, and had some very nice little neighborhoods, several of which did *not* fit in with the mostly nice, occasionally dicey, mix that I had seen in my previous stops. I rode for quite a long time this morning to the outskirts of town to see the fairgrounds.

I have never been to a county, big district or state fair. In fact, I have never really had any desire whatsoever to do so.

But I have seen fairgrounds in all but two of the places I have stayed, and I now think I'm going to have to do that. Have a corn dog, or a funnel cake, ride a not-so-safe-looking carnival ride, something like that. Sounds like a plan.

Just writing "funnel cake" makes me immediately need to explain that growing up in New England, we had funnel cakes, usually sold at the beach, but they weren't called that. In a refreshing burst of honesty, they were merely called "Fried Dough." I never really liked them much, but maybe now I'll have to give the more creatively named version a try.

I mentioned not going to a county fair. Where I was raised, the significance of the county you lived in was minuscule. I would say that more than half of the people in Massachusetts couldn't tell you what county they lived in. Most every town had a significant population and all of the services were town run. You had to commit a relatively serious crime to even go to county court. By the way, my hometown of Framingham was in Middlesex County. But you always had to think about it for a minute when you were filling out a form or something like that.

The first Thanksgiving that I was at the University of Kansas, I wasn't going to travel 1,500 miles for a couple of days visit home, but they did close the dorms, so you had to find a friend to be nice enough to have you as a guest. I received an invitation from a guy on my floor who lived in Anthony, Kansas. As we made the drive from Lawrence, at one point I asked him what town we were in. He replied that we were in such and such county. I again asked what town, and he said we weren't in a town. This was completely foreign to me. There was no "town" where I was from. You left one town, and then you were in another, and you sure didn't know what county that town was in.

I had a girlfriend when I worked in upstate New York, and she had been raised in the country, and had fun with my complete lack of understanding of things country. We were on the air together. She was a news anchor, and there would be some crosstalk. After one little discussion before my sportscast, I once again revealed my ignorance of anything related to farming. The next sportscast she introduced me as "Suburban-face Danny Clinkscale." Totally accurate.

This description further held true on the trip to Anthony, when after I had seen about three water towers in a half-hour or so, I asked what they were. The Anthony resident, fully delighted about how naïve I was about this stuff, replied that they were nuclear missile silos. I swallowed it whole until I had seen a couple more, and said, "C'mon, this would have to be the most protected state in the union." He couldn't maintain his stoicism anymore and burst out laughing.

· · · · ·

Today's destination was purely a matter of getting half of the 10 or so hours left to get home taken care of. That led to the choice of Hastings, Nebraska. I hope that there aren't many, or actually any, readers who are from this town. That's because I have to say that Hastings was easily the most disappointing stop of the journey. I'll get to that.

The drive to Hastings, however, was really nice and provided a perfect start to winding down my small adventure. Just because of the way it worked out and not by plan, I retraced steps from the beginning of the trip for about an hour or so in the Sand Hills. It shows how widening your horizon is interesting. It still was a scenic drive, but after what I had seen in South

Dakota, Wyoming, and Montana, had indeed lost a little panache.

I passed back through Broken Bow. It was early afternoon, and it was just a week since I had been there. It seemed much longer than that, and that was a good thing. It would not have mattered in my decision-making, but as it turns out, I forgot that tonight was actually going to be "The Big Kahuna" night that I had heard about last Friday at the Arrow Hotel. Perhaps I missed out on an epic time.

This portion of the drive, seeing some of the same places again, was kind of wistful. It really was a perfect way to start winding down and getting ready for the return to the regular rhythm of life. I smiled more than once thinking back to starting out on this journey with some wonder as to what would unfold, and the reality that it would be everything that I had hoped it would be.

I drove on to Hastings. It was the biggest town that I stayed in at just a touch under 20,000 citizens. That "large" a population meant that there was no small town charm to it. It had more chain stores and a large mall; things I had gladly been able to avoid even seeing, for the most part. Of course, having a large mall meant what it usually does, that the town had a rather depressed downtown area, the kind where about a third of the storefronts were vacant. It just generally had kind of a depressing vibe to it.

The saving grace was a little tour by car (I wasn't going to cover this whole town on a bicycle) I took around Hastings College. It was a truly lovely area, and it allows me to say something nice about the community.

In keeping with the general overall disheartening feeling was the motel. I'll just let it go unnamed because nondescript or worse would be the general description. Let's just say they did a dandy job on the website with their photos since it looked OK this morning when I decided on this destination. After my first five-hour drive in a few days, I pulled up and gave serious thought to changing my plans.

It had the look from the outside as the kind of place you would stick in a movie to show the seedy side of life. Throw in a couple of palm trees and some period detail and it would have fit right into a Raymond Chandler novel. But I was tired, and I'm not that picky about where I'm going to stay for a night by myself. Even if it was twice as nice, I still wouldn't have dreamed of staying there with my wife, which would be impossible anyway because we never would have gotten past check-in if we had been together.

The eventful check-in went like this. I was paying cash here (which I guess fits right in), and I gave the young lady a one hundred dollar bill for the $59.00 tab. She had to go find the manager to get the cash for change. The manager actually left the property to go get it. Ten minutes later, I had my change, and it made me wonder about the whole scenario of how and where he might have obtained it.

With some trepidation, I pulled up in front of my ground floor room with an outside entrance. Actually after the first three days, I had an outside entrance at every motel, which indicates what I was choosing, but for my purposes, was pretty convenient. About 50 yards away was the third consecutive well-advertised pool that sat empty of water on a hot, late spring day. *Not* adding to the ambiance was an old green hose that I guess was going to fill that pool up ... slowly ... sometime.

With the probably inaccurate, but tangible feeling that I was joining junkies and hookers as residents for the night, I opened the door with an actual key, not a key card. (It was the third time for that, by the way). It was with great relief that I found the inside was much nicer than the outside. Now that doesn't mean nice, but it was nicer, and acceptable.

I have traveled a tremendous amount as an adult, both the kind that I am doing right now, through small towns and staying in motels, and the more glamorous kind in big cities, in nice hotels. I can unequivocally say that this motel in Hastings might be in the running for worst I have ever stayed in, but not the winner.

I can't imagine that the place still exists so I don't feel bad in saying that the champion is (was?) the Jayhawk Motel in Marysville, Kansas. This came on a little sales trip I was making when I was working for a short time in Topeka. It was at a time of great transition in my broadcast career.

I lived in Utica, New York, for seven-plus years. The radio station WIBX was a tremendous breeding ground for major talent. Seven consecutive sports directors like me had gone on to do major league sports. Many of the others were major league play-by-play men. It was a great learning laboratory with talented and wonderful people. But it was *not* the type of place where you were supposed to work for over seven years. Despite constant attempts to move up the ladder, and many supposed "close calls," my first wife had had enough of the upstate New York winters and the long hours and low play. We had just had our first child, Cassady. She had earned the right to ask that we move closer to her roots back in Kansas.

We agreed that I would broadcast one more summer of baseball and she would move ahead to Lawrence and set up our new life. That summer bore no fruit professionally as far as advancement, and I joined them in the fall of 1994. That meant moving to a new area with no job, and in the broadcast profession maybe more than any other, that is bad business. You just scratched around to find something.

With the caveat that I would have to sell advertising time, I got a gig doing high school basketball for a fledgling operation that purchased time at one of those ultra right-wing radio operations that broadcast Art Bell types that believed in black helicopters and every other wacky conspiracy under the sun. Unlike most novice broadcasters, I had avoided having to do this, which is almost always a requisite at small stations. I'm not good at it, and I don't like it.

But you do what you have to do. I would sell the high school games over the phone, and then go to the businesses, meet the folks, pick up the copy, and get the small checks. I was on a little combination trip of broadcasting games and doing business in central Kansas, which lasted three days and would conclude in Marysville.

I was trying to save every penny, so in checking the local Yellow Pages (no internet of course) I saw an ad that touted the economic value of the Jayhawk Motel. I think even they didn't want to advertise the fact that they featured a $9.00 room rate, but when I drove up, that's what the sign said, and I bit.

Well, I got my money's worth. I slapped down a $10 bill and got change and a metal key, which I inserted in the door, and entered cautiously. It was a tiny room, but didn't look all that bad. I turned on the television to discover it was black and white. Yep, it was 1994, and I had a black and white, 14-inch TV.

It was late, and I went to bed on a not so great mattress. I

Downtown in Hastings, Nebraska, home of one of the worst *motels I've ever stayed in.* Wikipedia Commons.

can sleep on a bed of nails, so that wasn't a big deal. The next morning, I arose and went for a run. I hadn't noticed the night before, but when I went to take a shower afterward, I saw there was *no* shower curtain. I couldn't imagine what an ordeal it would be to get one, so I just decided to shower without it. I turned the water on, and the showerhead fell off. That meant a "shower" with water merely tumbling out of a spigot. Plenty of water got on the bathroom floor, but that was going to be their funeral. They had my $9, but I had a story and an easy champion for worst motel ever, to this day.

The return trip included an example of why I couldn't be a sales person. Most people in radio in their early jobs had to be sales people, but as I said, I had not had to do so. I was so busy at each stop, I wouldn't have had time anyway. I just broadcast for my pittance of a salary. But I was giving it a go at this job.

When you sold a sporting event for a high school broadcast, basically the business owner was just supporting the team. He knew that if we didn't get a certain level of sales, we just wouldn't do the game. The people who actually would have listened are at the game anyway so there was no real advertising value. So I didn't really feel too hot about the whole process anyway.

But on the way back, I stopped in a town where I forgot to pick up the check and the ad copy from a furniture store. As I drove up, I was greeted with store windows plastered with "Going out of Business" signs. I would find out in talking with the people that their Mom and Pop enterprise would be closing shop before the game broadcast would even occur. But they paid anyway, and I slunk out the front door not feeling real good about myself.

I drove down the road to a used car lot in Saint Marys, Kansas. It was just the kind of place that you wouldn't want to buy a car, and the owner was straight out of central casting for a used car salesman, right down to the plaid jacket. As we chatted, I received my payment and advertising copy, and I gazed around at clunkers that looked like they might not make it to the edge of town.

He asked me how I was enjoying doing the games, and I told him that I very much enjoyed doing play-by-play anytime. He then asked how I like the sales part and I told him I really hated it. He asked why, and I used the example of the place that I had just been, and the fact that I didn't feel like I was doing much of a service for the customers. His reply, "Aw, you can't worry about shit like that."

I'm pretty darn sure he didn't. I'm also sure that he had many a heated conversation with some poor sap who had bought one of his barely restored beaters that lasted about a week and died. Perhaps I was wrong, but I don't think so.

He didn't much seem to fit in what is one of the lovelier little towns around.

In not-as-lovely Hastings, it was about 3 o'clock and I needed a nap. I was thinking about perhaps playing golf, but decided that even a nice country course would just feel lame after yesterday. I really had the urge for a baseball game, and I thought maybe there was some level of pro or semi-pro ball in a town of this size. No dice there either. Then I thought maybe a cold beer at a nice outside patio might be enjoyable, but the spots that touted that online didn't pass the eye test.

Right down the road there was a sports bar that was large and had a lot of cars parked there, so I settled on that. Watch a ballgame, have a beer, and … play KENO? That certainly wasn't planned, since I had never played KENO and didn't know what it was exactly. But dozens of people inside certainly did. It apparently is a pretty big deal here in good old Hastings.

I got a table and sat down. I had to read the instruction sheet to figure out what to do. KENO is basically a bingo-like game run by the state, with drawings every 10 minutes or so. It's a pretty mindless enterprise, so I could play while watching the Royals and I wasn't going to gamble much anyway. As it turned out, in my first (and maybe last, who knows?) foray into KENO I won several times. After food and beverages, I left with over 50 bucks. Yessiree, Danny Clinkscale, the KENO king.

I figured there wasn't any way to top all that "excitement," so I returned to the shotgun motel, which didn't seem any more inviting at night, and called it a day. At least I knew that I had a color television, and that the showerhead wouldn't fall off.

13.

AGE 43
MILLENNIUM ROLLER COASTER

I think it is safe to say the second most significant year of my adult life was age 43, coming in a close second to age 26; 43 was an impactful year. I'd had some better years, but I didn't have any worse, and there was enough good so that the year was more impactful then dreadful. By the time that it ended, I was back on a nice course.

During this 12-month period, I would get divorced, see my children move nine hours away, get fired, quickly find another job, and then toward the end, meet the lovely lady who would later become my second wife. Besides that, nothing much happened.

I turned 43 as the millennium was about to conclude. It was a time when most people were thinking about potential Y2K disasters and the upcoming presidential election. My concerns were certainly not on the first issue, I'm not much of a worrier generally, and for the second, I sensed a bit of inevitability about the result.

As the year started, I was in my fourth year at KMBZ in Kansas City, and I liked my job and assignments. The company was terrible to work for, however. It was a giant conglomerate based in Philadelphia, and we would see the upper management about twice a year. To give you an indication of the corporation's attitude and the local management's treatment of their employees, I have a recollection of one time they were hosting corporate top dogs at the station. The newsroom was used to serve a buffet for all the visiting brass as they were touring the station. Nice, except that was where all the news and sports people were actually working. So there was a pretty fancy setup with big, giant shrimp and all, and employees not only weren't invited, but they had to watch without being allowed to take a bite.

On the whole, though, the people I worked with on a daily basis were almost all great. Many are friends and acquaintances to this day, and are talented and dedicated people. Ironically, several of them who were let go by the shortsighted conglomerate, now have successful careers at my current, much nicer home at WHB.

As I said, I very much enjoyed the work. My major assignments at that time were hosting the evening talk show from 6 to 9 p.m. as well as hosting the Kansas City Royals pre and postgame shows. I was also subcontracted to be the play-by-play announcer for KU women's basketball. When available, I also did postgame work for KU men's basketball coverage. Each of those assignments was generally great, but the subplots created major challenges.

I was the headliner for the talk show, and I worked extremely hard at making it something listeners would enjoy. Several different producers worked on the broadcast, all loving sports, radio, and taking pleasure in the show itself. They also all left after relatively short periods of time, because their dedication and skill were rewarded with near minimum wage pay and no benefits.

KMBZ was a news/talk station and only did sports from 2

p.m. until 9 p.m. or whenever a sports event ended. So the station was programmed by people who really were more news/weather/information oriented. This would create some very challenging shows. This was just before the heyday of sports talk hit, and in Kansas City, WHB would basically create that narrative.

KMBZ held the rights to Monday Night Football, postseason Major League Baseball, and other major events. But in all their wisdom, they didn't carry any of them. The program director wanted "local," and that often meant yours truly up against some of the biggest events in sports. Hey, I am a big fan of me, but the station deciding that my show was better radio than the World Series or Monday Night Football might give you an indication of how an opening was created for the gutsy, upstart station known as KCTE—later to become WHB.

Doing the Royals pre and postgame work was fantastic, even though the team was dreadful. It's far more fun now having a World Series winning team, but even with a bad one, it was a fine assignment. The hours created by this job were massive, and the pay was comical. At one point, out of desperation, I pitched a $4,000 annual raise. They came back with a final offer of $2,000, but only if I would expand from doing the weekdays' Royals shows, to all the games. So basically, there was no tangible raise, just more hours, and I had no choice.

The KU men's basketball coverage on KMBZ can be summed up in one story. My partner on the show was John Doolittle, a long time fixture in Kansas City broadcasting, one of the nicest men you ever had the pleasure to meet and a dedicated professional. This was a freelance assignment for him, and he does it to this day.

In 1999, Kansas was coming off a string of highly ranked teams that found major disappointments in the NCAA tournament. I was there when Kansas teams had been upset by Arizona in Birmingham in 1997, and in Oklahoma City in 1998 by Rhode Island. The night before the latter loss, many media members including John and I were taking a break at a country concert. Performing before the two-step dancing was an unknown group called the Dixie Chicks. They were fantastic and wouldn't be unknown for long.

KU did not have a typically vintage year in 1998-99, and drew a sixth seed in the NCAA tournament. Expectations were low. They were assigned to New Orleans in the first round. Since the station had done postseason coverage in the past, we just assumed we would do it again. But when initially approached, it was a no-go from management. Another attempted pitch failed. Only when we eliminated our airfare did they bite.

Driving to New Orleans was an epic haul in many ways, but we were up for it. As a final gesture, the program director (I'm being nice, he will go nameless again), ducked in the door as John and I were about to start our tournament preview show, after which we would start driving at 9 p.m. He told us not to mention on the air that we were driving, because it looked small time.

Perception over cheap reality.

The trip was quite the event. John was always a great traveling companion, when he got to go. The clear, cultural lowlight of this voyage was a stop at the very well-known Lambert's Café in Sikeston, Missouri, about halfway between St. Louis and Memphis. It's known as the "Home of the Throwed Rolls" because, yes, they do throw rolls to you as you enjoy family dining. Every time I traveled out of town, I liked to buy a trinket to take home to my little daughters. So, while John was enjoying a piece of pie I strolled into to the gift shop. I wandered over to the snow globes, and to my horror, there was a snow globe depicting a slave down on all fours getting whipped! I went up to the register and asked the checkout lady what the hell this thing was doing in their shop. She responded by saying "Why, it's just a cute, little snow globe." Resisting the temptation to toss the item through a window, I instead kept my mouth shut and put the wildly offensive object back on the shelf and tried to recover.

After staying at a casino in Mississippi, and other travel vagaries, we provided coverage for the first round game, which KU easily won over Evanston. Then we covered an early KU exit from the tournament, although the Jayhawks gave a spirited effort before falling in overtime to third-seeded Kentucky 88-92, in the second round. Then it was back on the road for the long drive home.

But through all these challenges, my co-workers at KMBZ and the work we did made it a rewarding job. There were also other radio stations at the complex, and the music station people were top-rate and fun to be around. We could all commiserate about those folks a couple of thousand miles away who knew nothing of our work, and just saw us as lines on a balance sheet.

As mentioned, my birthday is August 6, and my anniversary fell the day before. Leading up to that date, my wife Tracy and our two very young daughters were on a family vacation at Old Orchard Beach in Maine. I should have smelled trouble just before the trip when Tracy said that I shouldn't bother to plan anything special for our 10th anniversary and that the trip would suffice. I was oblivious, despite the struggles caused by split-shift working and the jobs we both had to have just to survive. By all surface evidence, everything was fine. I considered myself happily married and it seemed mutual.

More evidence should have come when during the trip; I went out on my daily run and came back very excited that, purely by chance, I had stumbled across the cabin we had spent our honeymoon at almost 10 years earlier. Tracy seemed mighty underwhelmed by this knowledge, even though she is a pretty excitable person.

The rest of my family had a 10-day trip, but that was too long for a KMBZ broadcaster, so I went home four days earlier. Tracy was around my family, whom she was very close to, and during those four days, there was no pressing news shared. Just a few days after the girls came home, I was at the ballpark for pre and postgame work. My phone went off just before the pre-game show and Tracy asked when I would be home. This was an extremely odd question since my usual routine after a game was that I would get home after midnight following the long postgame show and drive to Lawrence, Kansas, where we lived.

Even though she had to work early in the morning, she said she would be up. I asked if there was anything wrong and she replied that there was, but wouldn't specify. This had to be serious, so I said I would make arrangements and come home immediately. Yes, serious, but I can honestly say that if anyone at the ballpark had wanted to bet me all the money I had that I would soon be told I was going to be divorced, I would have gladly taken the bet. I would have lost. And for a while, I was lost.

I don't know how other people react mentally when they are told that their marriage is over, but at first, I felt as if it must be all my fault. I thought back to every little thing that might have changed the outcome. It took me a few miserable months to start to sort it out in a more reasonable way, and realize that there was blame to be shared, and maybe no blame at all.

But life was miserable. The one anecdote I will use to explain the depths of my despair was when I was searching for an apartment, and I settled on one north of the Country Club Plaza in Kansas City. It was a decent little place, but when it came time to sign the papers, I found myself unable to scratch out my signature. I couldn't stop thinking that I shouldn't even be there. I asked the lady for a couple of moments, and then I went out to the sidewalk and threw up. I eventually walked back in and told them I was backing out. I finally settled for a worse, but more reasonably priced, studio apartment quite close to KMBZ.

The radio station, and my nightly show itself, provided the best relief. I actually had to pretend to be in a normal frame of mind for three hours a night, and that was helpful. Slowly but surely, I started to feel better. I have been very fortunate to be a happy person almost my entire life. There was one period in my college years when I went through a bad spell that was far worse than this, so I did have the strength of realization that as bad as I felt, that feeling would eventually go away.

For several months, I didn't even give a thought to dating, but that came to an end in a somewhat unique way. I was making a 10-day work trip through Texas, a combination of KU women's basketball play-by-play, and men's basketball postgame reporting. The trip concluded in Austin, where I had never been. I was covering a Big Monday men's game between

Kansas and Texas. I arrived Saturday morning, so I had a couple of days off. While there, I used the gym often and you had to pass the reception desk to get there. Every time I passed for any reason, a pretty blonde lady with stereotypically big Texas hair would exchange very enjoyable pleasantries with me. It would turn out her name was Dolly. Dolly from Austin.

I still wasn't in the frame of mind to really engage in actual flirting, but Dolly was pretty relentless. On Monday when I went to lunch, I thought to myself that it was about time I got out of the mud and at least think about a date. Dolly would make that pretty easy. I had to book the hotel shuttle to go to the game, and she was the one who did that. She asked how I was going to return and I said I was just going to go out a bit on 6th street and would take a cab back.

In an extreme Texas drawl Dolly replied, "You mean, you're going to go out on 6th street and you're not going to ask me?" I stammered out something about the fact I would be working until midnight, and she said, "Well, that's fine. I'll pick you up then." In fact, when I came down to get the shuttle to go to the game, she said it was tied up and that she would take me ... in her red pickup truck.

Despite the fact I had an 8 a.m. flight, we closed down 6th street, and in fact, I never went to sleep. Dolly and I exchanged some letters and phone calls for a bit, but we never saw each other again. I had great support from family and friends during my "recovery" period, but nobody was more helpful than Dolly. Maybe somehow she will read this, and know how much she mattered.

After being depressed for a bit and you finally come out of it, you appreciate joy more. I now took pleasure in my freedom, but the adjustment that was most difficult was having my two lovely daughters far away from me. Their mom had almost immediately moved to Nashville, and that was tough. But I made it work. About once a month, I would fly to Tennessee for the weekend. I would either take Friday off, or if there wasn't a show on that date, I would create a long weekend.

I would pick up the kids, who were 2 and 6 at the time, and we would stay at a hotel Friday and Saturday nights. I returned them home late Sunday afternoon so they could attend school on Monday. I sometimes would visit them at school a bit before flying back. We had a lot of great, though brief times, and the leaving part was hard.

The first time I was there, I sat in on Cassady's class for a little while. Then it was time for recess, and time for me to say goodbye. I hugged her, lingering as long as I could, then went off to my rental car to drive to the airport. I turned right adjacent to the playground outside the school, only to see the heartbreaking scene right out of a sad movie, of her running down the fence line with tears streaming down her face, screaming at me not to leave. The image is burned in my brain.

But mostly my memories of the five years the kids lived in Nashville are good ones. That includes the Sunday nights I had to myself. Nashville is a superb music city, and not just for country music. There was the Bourbon Street Blues and Boogie Bar which I went to many times—great atmosphere and tremendous acts. There was just so much talent in the city.

There was another club off the downtown, the name of which I can't remember, but they had Sunday night broadcasts on the local NPR affiliate from that location. Usually the lead act was a singer/songwriter who had written hit songs for others. Those people would virtually always have a guest sitting in who was well-known. Vince Gill might be on guitar, or some standout session musician would be there. It was a wonderful experience. Maybe not surprisingly, I haven't been back to Nashville since my children moved back to this area, but my 50 or 60 visits were memorable.

Back home it was moving into summer, and this year was about to take another bad turn. The wonderful development of meeting my future wife, Jayne, was chronicled earlier, but she got an early dose of my profession as our relationship was just beginning. One week in July at KMBZ, the vibe was a little different. There had been some personnel movement there, and they had launched a fledgling all-sports station.

There were more sports employees around, and there was some other movement at KMBZ itself. I had failed in another recent attempt to get a paltry raise. Something just seemed funny. Finally, the program director asked me to come to a meeting later in the day. I smelled a rat, so I went to my then (and future) co-worker Soren Petro. I asked him if he knew what was up. He did a pretty nice and gutsy thing. He knew I was going to get fired (if you wanted to be technical, my contract would not be renewed). He knew, because he had a longer-term contract and was being moved to my slot. I had to keep it quiet until the meeting, which I did.

If you have ever walked into a meeting with your superior, and the HR person is there with a folder on her lap and a sheepish look on her face, don't expect good news. I had the goods anyway, but it was still pretty grim. The PR lady was (and is) a very nice person, and a friend, and you could tell she felt bad, as I had the news delivered by the program director.

Being an unemployed broadcaster is not an unusual status. My dad had a very successful career in radio and television. He had about 10 jobs and seldom left one on his own volition. Even at that point in 2000, I had left far more jobs on my own than I had been asked to leave, but still it's not fun, and finding new work is usually no picnic.

Luckily, this time that was not the case. Within 48 hours I had three strong opportunities. There were two minor league hockey play-by-play jobs available, one in Cleveland and one in Atlanta. Or, I could stay and work locally at WHB in Kansas City. The decision wasn't simple, but it ended up being a pretty easy call. I love play-by-play; it is what I would choose to do all the time in a perfect world, although I enjoy every area of broadcasting.

But staying in Kansas City had its allure in being close to my daughters, and I did have a good play-by-play assignment with KU women's basketball. WHB had approached me in the past, but I had been unsure that their effort to establish an all-sports radio station in Kansas City would succeed. They bucked a lot of odds in becoming a successful station, including being privately and locally owned. I was very fortunate that they still wanted me at the time I was in need of a new opportunity. Fifteen years later, it's been quite a run and a rewarding place to work.

I started the year married with one job and finished it unmarried (although pointed in that direction) with a new job. The time in-between was as much of a roller coaster as just about any year could have. Who would have guessed that 2014-15 could almost top it in dramatic fashion?

14.

Bad Rooster
and Good Vibes

June 6 - Day 9

Hastings, Nebraska to home (Shawnee, Kansas) 308 miles

Having dominated the KENO world and surviving the evening at my palatial motel, it was time for my final bicycle ride of the trip. Hastings has already taken some abuse from me, but the ride was a nice one. I saw some nice parks and neighborhoods that gave me a better feeling for the community.

There was yet another county fairgrounds to soak in, but perhaps the highlight of this beautiful June morning was a strange sight in an older neighborhood. In this particular area, track housing lined the streets and was probably built just after World War II or in the 1950s.

All the houses are very similar, but the backyard of one of them featured what, at first blush, appeared to be a smaller version of the home that had sunken into the ground up to the rooftop. It dawned on me when I saw the side entrance, that this was an underground bomb shelter. It was basically a small residence that a family could hunker down in when the "Big One" was expected to drop.

Just imagine—what kind of overwhelming paranoia gripped

our nation during the Cold War that convinced people in the middle of Nebraska to think that they needed this thing? The fact that Mr. and Mrs. Small-town America thought that the Russians would target this spot is pretty remarkable. It was an interesting historical window for me as I cruised back toward my final motel shower.

If I pushed it, I could be home in about five hours, but on this day, I was going to take my time. I let all the thoughts about how this journey had come about, and how it had gone, marinate. At the other end of the day's journey waited my beautiful wife, Jayne. She had, as I expected, completely understood my flight-of-fancy.

Our anniversary is tomorrow, 13 years for us. Like every couple, we have had our ups and downs, but far more of the ups. We met in 2000, and the story has a strong sports connection involving one of Kansas City's greatest sports legends, so it kind of fits here, and even if it doesn't, so be it.

I say we met in 2000, but that is not technically accurate. Our actual first encounter came when Jayne was working at an ad agency in Kansas City in the mid-1990s and running public relations for the then Senior PGA Tour event that also happened to be part of my reporting coverage. Then in 2000, Jayne started her own public relations firm, Venice Communications, won the PR work for the tournament again through her own company and a venue was set for us to meet again.

Jayne is very good at her job, and she was always thoroughly professional, including following through after tournaments to get feedback regarding the experience of the reporters. She was extremely friendly and chatty, and seemed to enjoy being able to converse with someone who had grown up in the east, where she had lived and gone to college for a year.

I was married in those first years, and happily so, and was always a bit confused by the length of our conversations post-tournament. I would find out later there was nothing really significant about it; she was just friendly and good at her job. This kind of follow-up was standard for her.

But as the tournament approached in 2000 I was not married, and after a bad adjustment period, I was having a lot of fun as a single guy. For all the best of reasons, that kind of fun was about to end. I had gone from not wanting to date at all, to enjoying the flirting process which had been in cold storage for about 10 years.

That was my mood when there was a media day for the tournament a bit ahead of the actual event. The person doing the PR was no longer just an attractive and efficient blonde, she was an attractive and efficient blonde that I looked at in a completely different light as a single man.

I had a nice conversation with her, but I had to leave the event early to return to work. I went over to apologize for that and then turned to leave. I only took a few steps before I turned back around again and made sure I caught her glance, and then I didn't stop staring. I was hoping she got some kind of good vibe off our few seconds of eye contact, and my hopes were eventually realized.

When the actual tournament arrived, we didn't get off to the greatest start. I wasn't real happy with the media parking. It was in an area of gravel and dirt which had been turned into a bit of a mud pit by the rain. So when Jayne asked about how everything was, I said, "Fine, except for your miserable parking." She says now that her general thought was, "Who does this guy think he is?" Well, I thought I was a guy who got bad parking.

We grew past that and started to do some mild flirting. We made a fun wager on the Preakness Stakes horse race and other stuff like that. Here's where Tom Watson comes in. Tom didn't have much of a round on the first day and so for Saturday's round he would have an early tee time. I was following the leaders who had teed off much later and when I made the turn with them, I see on the scoreboards that Watson was finishing a hot round that put him right back into contention.

I hustled into the media area and found Jayne. I gave her the "backdoor" phone number at KMBZ, where I was working then, and told her if she could get Watson to call in on that number to our weekend sports show, I would buy her three drinks. I then went out and finished up following leaders around the back nine.

When the rounds ended, I went into the media room, and once again found Jayne and asked if she had accomplished her assigned mission. She had failed, or more truthfully, Tom had not agreed, citing some cookout or something he had to get to. I told her she was down to two drinks.

The tournament ended the next day in very dramatic fashion. Dana Quigley spoiled the Kansas City party when he held off the charging Watson by sinking a birdie putt on the final hole to edge out a win by one shot. Even with the excitement of the golf tournament and my love of that game as a player, fan, and commentator, right then my mind was on something else.

Everybody was winding down after the final press conferences and awards, and I approached Jayne and asked her if she would still like to have those drinks. She said yes, and we went to O'Dowd's on the Country Club Plaza and sat on the deck and talked the evening away. I walked her to her car, and kissed her, and my single days were on their way to being over.

I had been very busy with the tournament, and obviously got home late that evening and went to work the next day without checking my phone messages, back when they were recorded on a little machine. Monday night after work, I checked and one of the messages was from Saturday night, Jayne reminding me that I still owed her two drinks.

To this day, I am so happy that I actually asked her out on my own volition, without the knowledge that she had given me a little prod with the message. I had done it on my own ... with a little help from Tom Watson.

· · · · ·

The final day's drive started and soon outside of Hastings, I approached the reoccurring theme of lovely countryside. I was very glad to get a last taste of the wide-open spaces after choosing a "too big" Hastings for the previous night.

Basically, every other day I would stop and buy something to eat in the car, which was still a bit of an adventure in itself, due to lack of choices that worked even now, due to my condition. Also, my drives were long and I didn't want to waste any time. Since this was my last drive and it wasn't that long, I was going to take it leisurely.

After a couple of hours, I came upon Superior, Nebraska. I really couldn't have picked a better spot to stop. A lovely, tiny American town with about 2,000 people living there. It is proud of its Victorian homes which have spawned a Victorian festival.

Part of its history that resonates with me is the fact that it is

The Bad Rooster, but honestly, I had a great American lunch in this restaurant.

one of the smallest communities ever to support a professional minor league baseball team, the Superior Senators. The team lasted a couple of years in the 1950s and was the first professional stop for Hall of Fame pitcher, Jim Kaat.

The small, downtown area has the usual current mix of places that are active, as well as empty storefronts, but on this Saturday, the hub of activity was a very plain restaurant called the "Bad Rooster." A large stuffed rooster who apparently is "bad" stands in the front window. There are about 20 tables with the kitchen in full view, and the main attraction is old western movies that are projected on the wall of the establishment.

The place was packed with residents of all ages, and was really fun for people watching. It was the kind of place where you order your food at the register and then they bring it out to you. The ladies who worked the crisp operation were super friendly, and the atmosphere in the restaurant was pure Americana. It was a very, very nice experience on the final day of a wonderful journey which now has just a couple of hundred miles remaining.

There was a mixture of wistfulness for me that this cathartic journey was coming to a conclusion and real excitement to see Jayne, and bring some of the feelings and lessons of the trip into the resumption of my day-to-day life.

I was soon on Highway 36 traveling across northern Kansas. I passed through Belleville, Washington and Marysville on a beautiful, sunny day. I did not stop in Marysville to see if the infamous Jayhawk Motel still existed. I was listening to the Champions League soccer final. The game between Barcelona and Juventus was tied as I was entering Seneca, Kansas, so I diverted off the road to see if there was some place to watch the end of the game. The pleasant little town was dead as a doornail, and Barcelona then scored the go-ahead goal anyway. I also realized that asking to watch a European soccer game in a tiny Kansas town might be a stretch.

I got back onto the rolling Highway 36 and as the miles to home shrank, I realized only nine days previously, I had set out from the even smaller Kansas town of Mayetta on my little odyssey. The reason for the journey was maybe more about the expectation rather than the actual excursion, but it gave me a diversion to think and dream about during a really tough time. The trip itself exceeded its goal exponentially.

Sure, Murdo and Hastings are places I wouldn't return to, but even they provided the memory of the motel proprietor clinging to life, and an impressive win at KENO. The landscapes of America were more amazing in their serenity and their rugged beauty than I could have imagined. And, I went six-for-eight in picking out my little spots to make a night's home, which is a pretty nice average.

The list of strangers to observe and speculate about became a live canvass for me, from the cigarette-ravaged waitress in Broken Bow, to the chunky chanteuses in Hot Springs, to the man in Pierre who seemed to want to recruit me to the circus.

Returning to my very busy world would be a bit jarring, having lived with no plan, no schedule, and no responsibilities for over a week. I recommend it highly to anyone, although the total solitude of most of the hours might not be everyone's thing. In nine days, I had one five-minute conversation with anyone I knew.

But I did experience hours of internal conversations with myself, and that has me ready to move forward. My plan worked out perfectly from the three months of musing, to the nine days of living it out. I wasn't quite ready for an interstate yet, so instead of taking Highway 36 to Saint Joseph, Missouri, and then south on Interstate 29, which would be the far, faster route, I jumped on little Highway 73 to drive through remote Kansas countryside.

Horton, Atchison, then Leavenworth, I was very close now. I didn't get on an interstate until I was 10 miles from home. Having purchased an anniversary present when I was in Pierre, I thought I was set, but then remembered I spaced out and forgot to get a card. I stopped at a Target store a few miles from home. I was back in suburban sprawl, and I didn't much like it.

It took me back a few days that I didn't want to forget, the beauty of four days of Sand Hills and Black Hills driving, then logistically having to pass through Rapid City, South Dakota,

Me and my wonderful wife, Jayne.

on Interstate 90 on the only stretch of superhighway driving I did the whole time. I felt trapped by the Best Buy, Bed Bath and Beyond, and Walmart signs, and I couldn't wait to get out. It was claustrophobic and confining and something even worse than that. Maybe that's why even Murdo looked good that day.

Now I was home in Shawnee, Kansas. It was a beautiful, early evening in June. The house looked welcoming and there would be a lovely wife inside that nice home. Jayne was the reason I had felt so strongly that taking this flight-of-fancy was right for me. I'm not sure how many wives would have been cool with this plan. I would hope many, but I'm not so sure.

Five minutes of conversation and a few texts was all the communication we had in nine days. I'm sure it was me over-analyzing, but there seemed a little trepidation in Jayne's eyes when I first saw her. A long embrace later, I was truly home.

I can't say tangibly that I was changed dramatically, but I was changed. Daring to do something that was selfish, but was built on the foundation of love and friendship and great support from others, was enriching. I do smile more at my own and others' foibles now. I do appreciate the little things in life more now. And the big things maybe don't seem so big anymore. Either way, it's time to get back to them.

Epilogue 1

... AND THERE WAS MUCH REJOICING

July 29 is looming. That's the day when I go back for my three-month evaluation, following a CT scan a couple of days before. I am feeling quite good now, although I never really felt that bad. Full taste has returned, which is rather delightful. There is still an issue with drier foods due to my lack of saliva, but generally, I am producing more as time passes, and am far less thirsty most of the time.

I do have to be careful when broadcasting. My throat can still be drier than it used to be, and I think my voice has lowered a bit. That is generally good, but I can indeed lapse into a more monotone type of speech. It has always been something that I have had to be aware of, because I am generally pretty low key. I try to make sure to be more warmed up, but it's easy to forget.

My post-radiation treatment life feels somewhat similar to my post-knee surgery life. When you haven't had a major surgery on your legs, you never have to think about walking properly. After knee surgery, I am often aware of walking, of striding properly and of not lapsing into limping without even realizing it. It is the same with speaking. My dad taught me very well about breathing technique when I was very young, so it became second nature. Not now. You can believe that everything is the same, but it's not.

Even though I can eat just about everything I want, it is rather difficult to change over 30 years of learned behavior of always eating healthy. I've enjoyed a nutritional and light diet and always paid close attention to avoiding wildly, fatty foods. But I lost quite a bit of weight during the treatment, when I probably only needed to drop a few pounds. So I'm sure for most, there is envy that I have to gain weight, which for all of my life was something that could happen easily to me if I wasn't diligent with my exercise and diet.

Here's how easily I could gain weight back in the bad old days. When I was about 20 years old and taking some time off from college and living back at home, I got a part time job at a radio station in Marlboro, Massachusetts. I would do little things like man-on-the-street interviews, even did some movie reviews. I also filled in once when the morning newsman went on a three-week vacation.

I was not a daily exerciser then. The job entailed rising at 4 a.m. and on the way to work, stopping off at the Dunkin' Donuts to pick up the first edition of the local newspaper, since that was how you got the news to broadcast. I also needed to pick up donuts for the staff. Of course, I would eat a couple. Then after the 7:30 news, you returned to the Dunkin' for the later edition of the paper to see if there was fresh news. That of course, meant more donuts.

It was only a three-week stint as the morning-drive news-man, but I "larded" on 21 pounds in that span. You do the math, about a pound a day. Not long after that, I would change my ways. I had often yo-yo dieted since I stopped growing, and I was good at losing weight ... and gaining it back. I was sick of that cycle and went on kind of a permanent semi-diet, so I would never have to go on a full-blown diet again.

Human beings are funny creatures. I had probably eaten ramen noodles no more than three times in my life prior to treatment. But they became a staple when they were about all I could stand and had a consistency that I could handle. But I really grew to like them, and somehow they are still something I very much like to eat. That's not a bad thing, because they are so cheap, they just about give them away.

That's not the case with some other items that I had to force down during the process. At first, I had to go with protein shakes, and I always did chocolate. Then I advanced to real chocolate ice cream shakes. I have grown so sick of them that I've switched to strawberry. I liked strawberry ice cream from about age 8 to 10, but after that, never. Now the guy at the Dairy Queen across from WHB starts making a small strawberry shake, extra strawberries, before I get through the door.

• • • • •

So with three weeks before the big medical day and one month past the cathartic road trip, it's time for another small excursion. Thankfully, the Kansas City Royals will provide the conduit for the trip. Their great success has made extra work for all of us, but it's great extra work. The Royals have usually been a non-story by Memorial Day, and certainly have become irrelevant in our world when the Chiefs' training camp gets underway. Not now. Extra shows, extra emphasis, and for me, extra assignments like the excitement of the World Series and now, the All-Star Game.

The Royals are sending seven players, their manager, and a bunch of staff to Cincinnati, so it's a big deal. My wife has great friends who have a beautiful house with guest accommodations in the Queen City, so I am going to stay there, which saves the company a few bucks. I also said I would drive it. My work would start on a Monday, so I decided to make the trip a little odyssey again.

I would drive part of the way, stay over, and then drive the rest on Sunday. I wanted a destination similar to what I had experienced last month along the way with a place to play golf. About 30 miles off the regular interstate route is the town of Mattoon, Illinois. My wife makes the same drive to go see her friends and rehearse her opera singing with her friend and collaborator, Thom. She usually stops in Effingham, kind of a popular place for layovers because it's at the junction of I-70 and I-55. I wanted something about that distance away from home, but not so commercial and overblown.

A little research found Mattoon, a bit off the beaten path, but not far off the direct route either. It bears strong similarities to Broken Bow, and Belle Fourche, etc., similar haunts from the previous trip. The golf course looked nice out in the country, and it was big enough to have accommodation choices, with maybe a little something going on a Saturday night.

Days Inn was the choice, a company that has gobbled up some of the old Holidome properties that were all the rage back in the day. That's what this Days Inn was. They seem like a bad idea now, cool then, tacky presently, and if you're traveling alone as an adult, you pay the price for the low rate with the knowledge you are likely to get a kiddie pool party right outside your walkout window ... and I did.

Mattoon, Illinois, also seems like the most unlikely place for a bagel festival, but while I was staying at the Days Inn, the motel was the place where they were doing the interviewing and hiring for "Bagelfest." I was pretty much mystified at how one of the most urban of foods, had this event in little Mattoon, complete with Miss Bagelfest, and Beautiful Bagel Baby.

It turns out that Lender's Bagels started in Mattoon and that when owner, Murray Lender, first opened his bagel factory there, he would serve a huge bagel breakfast to advertise his product. And that was the derivation of the eventual "Bagelfest," which this year celebrated its 30th anniversary, and which I missed by a week. Too bad, I love a good bagel.

I love a good country golf course too, and the Fox Prairie course in Mattoon fit the bill. It would be a nice solitary few holes late on a Saturday, since it looked like it was going to rain for sure. It never did, and I had a really good time.

I was trying to cram in a whole lot in a little time. I basically was trying to duplicate what I had done on the big trip. One thing that has come of that cathartic experience is that it was so special that it's hard to duplicate, but the things I did were very enjoyable, and its simple pleasures can be repeated. Every long drive, every little town, every "Bagelfest," every "Big Kahuna Night," puts a smile on my face.

Heck, even bad karaoke does that. I'm not a fan. I've never sung. I have always generally thought it was kind of dumb. But things have changed. I always enjoy people watching, and I have always enjoyed watching people have fun. But now, I have a little different attitude. Instead of internally mocking someone croaking out "Hit Me with Your Best Shot," I kind of get a kick out of someone just having fun.

That particular song was part of the show at The Castle Inn bar in Mattoon that July Saturday night. After the evening golf,

I went back to the motel, showered up and Google-searched my way to this rather small, but lively spot. It was pretty late when I arrived and the rather country-oriented crowd was pretty well oiled up already. The courage level was high, and there was a nice parade of people who "performed."

I have never been bothered by being a loner in a bar, even if I become aware that others seem quite aware that I am something of an interloper. Most of the people on this night seemed to know each other quite well, and I'm sure they were aware I wasn't a "Matoonian" (if that's accurate, it's an accident). Either way, it didn't matter; I had fun and stayed until pretty near closing time.

I still managed to get up at a decent hour, since I was looking forward to getting in a pretty long bike ride before I had to check out of the motel and hit the road. Good thing I didn't sleep in. Mattoon isn't all that small a town and I rode around it quite a bit and went to the edge of the city where Routes 45 and 16 intersect. Somehow, I got a bit turned around and lost my bearings as to where my motel was. I was almost getting to the point where I was going to ask directions, when I saw, you guessed it, "The Castle Inn." It looked quite different in the daylight, but I knew how to get "home" from there, about 10 hours later than the previous time.

I was now on to Cincinnati for the All-Star Game. Covering an event like this, solo, for my radio station, is a lively combination of great fun, fulfilling work, and long hours. There were three daily local shows, plus a nighttime show that was on most evenings, and I broadcast them all. They were all different, and I tried to bring all the best sports information plus maybe some fun sidelights that kind of fit each show's personality.

In one case at the Midsummer Classic, our morning show guys discussed the quality of the iconic "Skyline" chili. The general consensus was that this unique-to-the-Queen City-style chili was not up to its outsized reputation. My general on-air persona through the years has been of someone who wouldn't go near something like chili, no matter what kind.

Now with taste buds having been restored post-cancer, weight to be gained, and an attitude to embrace some things I wouldn't have before my new lease on life, I volunteered for a chili tasting. When I was young and ate everything in sight before changing my ways, I very much liked chili. But "Skyline" chili is unique. It's generally served over spaghetti with shredded mozzarella on top, sauce that's kind of thin, and hamburger that is ground up pretty fine. My consensus for our listeners was that the hometown sensation was just OK. No, you don't have to have it when you go to Cincinnati. I was glad to check another box on things that I would now embrace.

The assignment for the game was in place because the event was so dominated by the Kansas City Royals, a far cry from the days when the Royals only had an All Star because it was a rule that every team be represented, and their selection was often quite an embarrassment. The Royals' players and management were rightly basking in the glow of their accomplishments.

For me, it was great fun to see all of the greatest players in the game, particularly some of the young new stars, and their reaction to their relatively newfound fame. As I went from table to table trying to grab interviews, I was quite impressed with how they handled the situation, and I found it refreshing to see how excited they truly seemed to be.

The Chicago Cubs' Kris Bryant answered one question with a remarkable fact that resonated with me. When I was a young ballplayer, our Little League team would play a couple of practice games, 18 regular season games, two a week, and then a handful of playoff games. I was on the All-Star traveling team, but we maybe only played 10. So in a summer, I might have played 35 games tops. When Bryant was 10 years old, he estimated that he played 185 actual games!

It was all quite fun, from the Home Run Derby to the game itself, which was won by the American League, meaning their champion would have home advantage in the World Series. Royals' manager, Ned Yost, was the All-Star skipper, and he had made winning the game a priority, in part because he knew his club could be the beneficiary of home field. It hadn't worked out the year before when the Royals lost game seven at home, but maybe this year it would.

I had designs on driving the entire way from Cincinnati back to Kansas City, but on that Wednesday, I eventually decided to stop just east of Columbia, Missouri, in Boonville. There is an Isle of Capri casino and hotel there, and they had a special weeknight rate, so I decided to make things a little easier, and slip in a little evening golf, too.

I have actually stayed in Boonville several times through happenstance in my travels and also while covering sports events at the University of Missouri in nearby Columbia. It's an interesting place. It has seen good times and bad times, and its river location makes for an interesting history, and some nice scenery. It was a fun place for a run back in my running days, and now, for a bike ride near or along the Katy Trail.

Usually, I have not stayed at the casino, but this time I am.

I have been there a few times. I am not that much of a casino person, but when I have traveled to smaller places without much nightlife, I have found that at least there will be some activity at a casino, no matter how small.

I find most casinos, particularly the smaller ones, on the whole, to be fairly depressing places. There appears to be an awful lot of people who seemingly don't have much else to do, except play the mind-numbing slot machines with cigarettes in hand and frowns on their faces. While the tables (if anyone is using them) provide a more collegial, party atmosphere, I don't much see the fun in the slots, particularly the penny or five-cent variety, where hours of even successful play might net $2.00. However, I very much enjoy observing human nature, and there is plenty of that at any casino.

July 29 has arrived. It is six months since my surgery, and a little more than four months since I concluded radiation treatment. I feel good, I can eat anything. I'm exercising more vigorously. All seems well. But after doing extensive CT scans leading up to meeting with the radiation oncologist, it naturally makes one a little nervous heading into the six-month review.

My wife, Jayne, accompanied me and my wonderful doctor, Dr. Shen entered the room with the nurse, and a few other professionals observing. Having more people in there made it seem more ominous for some reason. Dr. Shen started to go through some pieces of information that seemed important and positive, but he had not really *said the words*. I finally interrupted some of the medical conversation and just bluntly said, "So, I'm OK?" He seemed a little surprised and kind of offhandedly said, "Oh yeah, sure," as if that went without saying.

While I was very optimistic, knowing was an unbelievable feeling. There are no guarantees, but it is exhilarating. It's funny, though, I obviously didn't want him to say that there had been a recurrence, or that they hadn't gotten everything, but my first concern was that I just didn't want to do that damn treatment again. And for the time being at least, I don't.

There was a funny moment to follow. Dr. Shen indicated that I would have another follow-up in six months, but noted that I would not have to have any scans at that time. He is not a native speaker, although his English is almost perfect. But there are nuances that escape anyone in that category. He said that at the follow-up visit he would only need to "feel me up." I asked him if he would like to rephrase that, and the whole group howled with laughter. But he still didn't quite get it.

I went outside on a beautiful sunny day, and looked around with much the feeling that I had on the days of my trip, soaking in even the simplest things. One simple detail was that I had to go to work. I got in my car and turned on the radio to our station, and they were discussing the news that Chiefs' safety, Eric Berry, had been ruled cancer free. He had Hodgkin's disease, and his treatment had been far more extensive than mine. But I knew just how he felt.

Arriving at work, I entered the office of my friend and host of the show where I do most of my work, *Between the Lines*, Kevin Kietzman. He and our producer, Todd Leabo, obviously had been in the group of only three who had known about the plans for my trip. In the subsequent months after my treatment, I had not discussed the issue directly on the air. Kevin had made a couple of nicely vague comments about me being tough through some medical issues, but cancer was not mentioned.

I walked into the office and announced, "Eric Berry isn't the only one having a great &%$&*#@ day." As they say in *Monty Python and the Holy Grail* ... and there was much rejoicing! Kevin suggested that given the circumstances, this might be the day to talk about it publicly. Given that I would have to speak to Berry's situation, he was right.

Kevin gave a very gracious introduction, highlighted by pointing out the thing I was most proud of, that I had worked every day through my treatment. He pointed out that many of my co-workers would have forgotten I was going through radiation except when a certain assignment had to be switched up due to the time of day conflict of my various treatments and appointments. Then we proceeded on to the decision to make the trip, and when it came to discussing the support of my wife, and my trust in her to understand the "secret" nature of it, I lost it on the air. I couldn't quite get through the part where I said how much I loved her, without breaking down.

I recovered relatively quickly and moved on through the 25-minute segment. Dozens of people called the show, and literally hundreds of people emailed me, many detailing how they had to pull over in their cars because they were overcome with emotion. Many of those people either had gone through the same thing or had family members who had, some not as fortunate as me. I was able to at least send a thank you to everyone.

It was incredibly gratifying, and made me happy that I basically had completely changed my mind about going public about this, and had provided a service to many in doing so. Something very good came out of something not so good at all.

EPILOGUE TWO

COMPLETE CLOSURE

It is October 27, 2015, exactly one year since I sat in the Parking Spot at Kansas City International Airport, and idly scratched my face, discovering the cancerous lump that would change my life. That was after returning from San Francisco and Game 5 of the World Series, which the Royals would lose to the Giants.

I covered every game of that wild ride through the playoffs, and as the Royals return to the World Series this year, I am also along for this one, which has been and will probably continue to be wilder. The Royals were left for dead at least once each year, in 2014 during a Wild Card single elimination game, trailing 7-3 in the bottom of the eighth inning, and again by a run in the 12th, only to dramatically prevail and then roll on to the Series.

This year they appeared doomed to early elimination again in their Division Series with the Houston Astros in game 4. The Astros were poised to send the Royals packing, leading 6-2 in the bottom of the eighth, up two games to one.

As I mentioned earlier, I have been an Astros fan since I was about 12, although I went to school at KU. Still, I always rooted for the Royals as my American League team. The Astros of course, are now in the American League too, and they have tenure for my fanhood.

So as the Astros pummeled a couple of homers to pad their

The Royals and Astros before the start of game 4 of the 2015 ALDS. Kansas City pulled off a magical comeback to win, 9-6, starting their run to the 2015 World Series championship.

lead in the seventh inning, Minute Maid Park was electric. The roof was closed and the sound of the celebrating fans was thunderous. In keeping with my cancer-recovery-fueled-resolve to soak in each moment more than ever, I looked all-around the park and watched the celebration with a special feeling. It appeared the Astros would win their first playoff series in a decade, and do it just removed from being the worst team in baseball.

But the Royals were the predecessor to the Astros in this regard, making the World Series in 2014 not far removed from being a laughingstock themselves. The defending American League champions were not going to die quietly. In the span of about 10 minutes, the Royals transformed Minute Maid Field from a cross-cultural dance club into a funeral home. Five rat-atat singles and a huge error on a double-play ball by the Astros' star shortstop, Carlos Correa, roared the Royals from doom to the lead. They would go on to win 9-6 and save their season. It really was amazing to witness it, emotions reversing stunningly in virtually the blink of an eye.

It was no surprise to anyone that although there was still a game to play back at Kauffman Stadium, the Royals had secured the series and a deciding Game 5 rout proved formulaic. The Royals were poised to take on the Blue Jays in the American League Championship series.

There was really no stopping the Royals now. They took the first two games of the series at home. In Game 2, the second of what would be eight stunning comeback postseason wins, was due to a botched pop-up by the Jays. So in winning fashion, the Royals were off to Canada for the next three games.

I had not been back to Toronto since I barely saved my running streak in the airport back in 2000. Toronto is a huge and remarkable city. I have been to New York, London, and Paris, and they are the most international cities I have ever seen ... until now. Toronto is an incredible melting pot of cultures and really just a fascinating place. I would love to go again soon with some time on my hands. The area near my hotel seemed more like Tokyo than Canada, and when I watched election coverage during the series, there were local results from the suburban town of Brantford, and the head shots of all the candidates on television featured a turban on virtually every one.

The tipping point Game 2 of the series proved vital, as Toronto took two of their three home games, all of which were decisive for the winning team, and the Jays had really needed them all. Returning to Kansas City, Toronto must win both games. They didn't even get the first, falling in the sixth game. The Royals, who had used their extremely close call in the 2014 World Series as a rallying cry all season, would get to go back and give it another crack.

A surprise opponent was waiting in the form of the young and swaggering New York Mets. Fueled by their fireballing, long-haired starting pitchers and the record-breaking post season slugging of Daniel Murphy, they seemed on a Cinderella-roll to a potential title. They were another franchise that had been miserable recently, and their fans had been reborn.

The Mets also had a seemingly impregnable closer in Jeurys Familia, who hadn't blown a save since May. But this is the 2015 Kansas City Royals we are talking about here, so of course, when Familia had the chance to close out a key Mets win in the first game of the World Series, he was victimized by Alex Gordon's game-tying home run in the ninth inning, and the Royals would win in extra innings.

The series opener did indeed fall on the anniversary date of my cancer discovery, but in retrospect, I don't recall actually thinking about it at the time. Blowing Game 1 became all the more glaring when the Royals routed the Mets in Game 2, and so it was off to New York with the Royals in the driver's seat once again.

The five days I would spend in New York were five of the craziest, most frustrating, funniest, most gratifying professionally, and just generally nutty as you can imagine. It started almost from the very minute the journey began, when I was bumped from my early morning flight to New York due to over booking. I would get on the next flight a little over an hour later, which wasn't so bad, although it would be a tighter schedule to get to Citi Field for off-day press conferences in the late afternoon.

Next up on the calamity list was the fact that when I arrived at LaGuardia Airport, my luggage was nowhere to be found, and that included the broadcasting gear that was vital. I usually carried it on, but there was no overhead space, so they gate checked it. I found the baggage folks and they told me my luggage was at the terminal where my original flight was supposed to land. I went running over there, and thankfully the little yellow case containing the radio equipment was sitting there. That was nice, but my other piece of luggage with everything necessary for a five-day stay was not.

A crummy situation, but I figured it would be the usual routine of filling out the paperwork, and after working for a few hours at the ballpark, I was assured that the bag would be at my hotel. When I got to the hotel about 8 p.m. and checked in, I found that my bag had not been delivered. I called the airline, and they said they were still trying to locate it. They never would. All I had were the clothes on my back, so I had to think quick. It was about 9 p.m. now, so I figured I would just hustle into Times Square and pick up a few necessary items. Well, it may be the city never sleeps, but that doesn't mean that clothing stores stay open all night. I had no success in getting something reasonably priced just for a day or so to work in and also for working out. I was still holding out hope that I would get my bag eventually, and I didn't want to buy a bunch of extra stuff I didn't need.

I headed back to my hotel, which was ideally located about halfway between Times Square and Citi Field. It was in a nice little neighborhood in Queensborough, right across from a train stop. I took a walk to get the lay of the land. I noticed that there was a Korean thrift shop almost directly across the street. So my plan for the next day was to take a flyer on that place, and then probably have to head back into the city, since it was becoming increasingly clear, I would need many items.

I went back to my hotel room and got set to go to bed, already mighty frustrated with how things had gone on this day. I took out my toothbrush and started brushing. Almost instantly, half of one of my front teeth broke right off. It was a very visible one right smack in the smile zone. I looked like a jack-o'-lantern.

So here I was in New York City, preparing to not only broadcast on the radio, but also do nightly television appearances on the NBC affiliates' sportscasts. I had no change of clothes, and I would have to try and keep my mouth half-closed on camera—delightful.

My wife had heard most of the story, but had gone to bed before the tooth fiasco. I texted her before I went to a fitful sleep, a message she would get upon arising. It said "It's a good thing I am not packing a gun, or I would shoot myself."

The worm would start to turn the next morning. After appearing on WHB's morning show, I walked across the street to see if anything of worth was in the Korean thrift store. Jackpot. Though a tiny little store front, it was stuffed full of everything. Suit coats, dress pants, ties, socks, underwear, workout gear. Everything except sneakers. It took about an hour to wade through it and get reasonable sizes, but I ended up with three suit coats, three pairs of pants, three pairs of socks, a three pack of briefs, three ties, workout pants, a belt, and two T-shirts.

Total price … $91.00.

That was obviously a steal, but the catch was that they didn't take credit. I had enough cash, but I would have been left without much. I was in the city, but had also given thought to visiting my parents in Boston, if the series ended in four or five games. So, I thought to myself, I'm in New York, and given the nature of the establishment, why don't I just try bartering. It was a good plan, and it was funny, too.

The male proprietor who had been helping me with selections had left to run an errand, and his wife was working the register. She spoke precious little English, which is fair, since I don't speak any Korean. The exchange went this way:

"How about 70 bucks for all of it?" I asked.

"$90," answered the lady.

"$75."

"$85."

The Korean Thrift Store. If you were looking for bargains, this was the place to go.

Then we batted the $75 and $85 back and forth at each other for a few volleys, and she finally said, "$80." I told her to ditch one of the pairs of pants, which was three bucks, and walked out with a brand-new wardrobe for $77.00.

I love New York.

I got a pair of athletic shoes in Times Square at lunchtime, and I was good to go on the day of Game 3 of the World Series. The Mets won the game handily and one of the major story lines was Mets' pitcher, Noah Syndergaard throwing high and tight at Royals' shortstop Alcides Escobar. Escobar had been one of the keys down the stretch and in the post season in the leadoff spot for the Royals. A player who didn't fit the leadoff role in any conventional baseball way, Escobar had turned up his nose at convention by swinging at the first pitch of the game no matter what, and he was open about doing it.

Stunningly, pitchers continually threw him good pitches to hit in the situation, and he thrived. It had gotten so absurd that at the previous day's press conference I had asked Syndergaard about it, and he replied that he had something special cooked up. The official World Series film included the response, including my question, which is kind of neat.

Just like the Jays, to realistically think they could win the Series, the Mets pretty much had to take all the games in their home park. As Game 4 moved along, it looked like they were headed another step in that direction. But instead, it was time for another dose of Royals magic, at the expense of another Mets postseason star.

Daniel Murphy was the National League Championship Series Most Valuable Player, and the selection wasn't close. He batted over .500 and hit four home runs, running his postseason total to a staggering seven. His offense had led the Mets to their upset of the Cubs. But, he has never been known for his glove at second base.

The Mets were up 3-2 in the top of the eighth inning. The Royals had two men on with one out. Eric Hosmer grounded to Murphy, who was thinking double play, when he had no chance at it. Under his glove it went, and the error fueled a 4-3 Royals' win. On this Halloween night, the Royals were one step away.

East coast baseball means late night World Series games and after postgame work and a packed train ride back to my hotel, it was after 1 a.m. But what the heck I thought, it's New York City and it's Halloween, and Times Square is a 10 minute cab ride away. It'll still be hopping. The City was only just starting to wind down, and seeing Pocahontas and Spider-man walking arm-in-arm was among the things that made it worth the trip.

I got back to the hotel about 3 a.m. so it was already Sunday, November 1, a date that Kansas City Royals fans now will never forget. I left for Citi Field about 2:30 p.m., so I had time to meet my great friend, Adam Shapiro, for brunch in Times Square. I realized on my way there that I would be leaving New York the next day, and I didn't have a suitcase. I also wanted to buy a nicer shirt for the TV broadcast that night.

So my afternoon, on what would turn out to be quite a historic sports day for Kansas City, was some quality time with a friend, a little shopping and then wheeling my newly-purchased large suitcase onto the subway to go back to my hotel. A change of clothes and I was back on the train for the trip to what would become the final game of the baseball season.

The Mets needed a win to force the series back to Kansas

City. For me, it would be a flight back to KC, or perhaps if all worked out, a train up to Boston to see my family. Once again, it appeared that one scenario, the trip to KC, was going to play out as the Mets' Matt Harvey was shutting down the Royals, with the Mets leading 2-0 after eight innings. But the Royals know how to flip any script, and they would do it one more time.

One more dose of magic began with Mets' manager, Terry Collins deciding not to do his job. He had decided to take Harvey out of the game and lean on his great closer, Familia. It was the right move, but Collins let Harvey talk him out of it. About two minutes later Harvey would be out anyway, having given up a walk, a double and a run.

Familia did his job. He threw two grounders, the first moved Eric Hosmer to third, and the second was another out that should have left Hosmer still at third. But David Wright, the Mets' third baseman, checked Hosmer at third for too long, and then "lollypopped" his throw to first. Hosmer took off, and many people thought he was a sure out (I didn't. I thought it would be close). But Lucas Duda, the Mets' first baseman, made it irrelevant by heaving the ball over the catcher's head, as Hosmer scored the tying run.

The game was only tied, but Citi Field felt and sounded about the same as Minute Maid Park had three weeks before. There was a sense of inevitability even though the Mets were at home. Those of us who had seen the Royals every day had an ever deeper sense of it. It took until the 12th inning, but the Royals then exploded for five runs.

I only saw the first one score. Once the Royals got the lead, with their flawless closer, Wade Davis, the game was almost certainly won and I had to get downstairs to the clubhouse. It was a weird scene, all of the media waiting to cover another Champagne celebration. But as the Royals continued to score, and then Davis struggled a bit in the bottom of the inning, we cooled our heels in a basement hallway for about a half-an-hour.

Finally, we saw on our phones that the game was over and soon we heard the sounds of wild celebration in the clubhouse. Champagne celebrations may be fun for the players and look like lots of laughs for fans, but they are no fun to cover. In fact, when I think about it, the reason for my half tooth was from getting bumped in the mouth by a TV camera during the ALCS.

Many of the camera people and others had ponchos or rain gear, and goggles and the like. My strategy was to work the periphery during the real mayhem, and sneak into the quieter sectors when possible. But it's impossible to not end up at least a little bit sticky with stinging eyes. When it's a World Series' celebration, it's work, but it's special. The joy of seeing people celebrate reaching the top of their profession is something. But the Champagne part, not so much.

There would be no early morning trip into Times Square ... befitting the occasion, WHB would broadcast all night long. I made my last appearance at 4:15 a.m., delighted to be sharing the air with the guys from our morning show, including one of the co-hosts, Steven St. John. Steven is a wonderful guy, he got into the radio business as a fan, and a great part of his appeal and charm is that he has remained a die-hard fan.

It's not an approach that I would, or could, pull off, but it fits him like a glove. On this overnight, delightfully over served, he reflected perfectly the joy, exultation and yes, relief of the long-suffering Royals fans. They had seen far too much bad baseball. Among the true events of previous seasons included a left fielder getting hit on the head by a routine fly ball that would have been the final out causing their 11th straight loss on the way to 19 in a row; a center fielder climb the wall in pursuit of a fly ball that landed 20 feet short of him in the field of play, and a first baseman beaned from behind by a relay throw.

But now 30 years removed from their last title, the Royals and their fans were champions. I had suffered along with them, doing pre and postgame shows every year since 1996, desperately hoping that someday discussion of the finer points of each game would have some meaning. I keep a meticulous large score sheet designed for extra note taking for every game I cover, and now it finally wasn't merely an absurd exercise.

Starting at about 4:30 a.m., I mixed little bursts of sleep with appearances on our shows, and then taped some things for *Between the Lines*, my daily main show. My friends at the station had gladly accepted my request for a few days off to go to Boston and see my parents, so I got on the Acela Express train late in the afternoon, weary but extremely satisfied. Gazing out the window at the passing landscape, I was nearing full circle on my World Series to World Series year of wildly fluctuating circumstances and emotions.

I see my parents perhaps once a year, probably a little less, usually coinciding with some birthday or anniversary. The Royals' wild card rally in 2014 had caused me to miss a trip with my wife and daughter for my mother's 80th birthday. So it was fitting that baseball caused a convenient little excursion up to suburban Framingham, Massachusetts, to the home where I grew up and my parents still live.

As I started a brief but delightful few of days lunching with my parents and my brother, John, 1500 miles away in Kansas City, the city gathered, 800,000 strong, for the parade and concluding ceremony at Union Station for the conquering World Series Champions.

Among the throng were my wife and our friend Linda. Linda is the kind of long-suffering die-hard Royals fan that made up a portion of the massive crowd. My wife represented the type of phenomenon that a winning sports team can create. Jayne is a successful businesswoman as well as an accomplished opera singer. She has always enjoyed sports a little bit, and now probably a little bit more, since it is my profession.

But like thousands of others who didn't really know a thing about cut fastballs or WHIP or double switches, she got swept up in the hysteria. I felt like I was in some kind of alternate universe while I was covering games and I would receive texts from her expressing the common Royals fans' complaints about Fox announcer, Joe Buck, reviled by Kansas Citians.

The parade however, took the cake. She and Linda maneuvered around Kansas City with craft, creativity finding a prime spot quite near the stage, just behind some people sitting in lawn chairs so they could breathe, it was so tight. This took hours and hours. Truly amazing, and a reflection of what a sports team can do for a city.

On Wednesday, I went for a long morning run and returned to see my 84-year-old dad out in the backyard raking and piling up leaves. He had been at this sporadically, apparently for a week or so. I joined him and we had a good chat and worked together for about a half-an-hour before he wearied a bit, and said he wanted to lie down for a minute.

Me and my dad.

Two hours later, while he slept, the job was done and the leaves were all sent to the woods. It was fun to see him arise and start to head to the backyard and to be able to stop him and tell him we could just sit down and have some lunch. Dad has lost some of his zip and bluster, but seeing him is always a treat. Lots of the same stories and quirky behavior that once might have been a bit annoying, now make me smile.

My mom is a delight. She has always been an extremely down-to-earth, thoughtful, and quiet person, but underlying that is a strength and impact that is palpable. A woman of great faith, she lives that rather than preaches it, and has a far greater effect on those around her than mere words can carry. Keeping the crazy bunch of eight Clinkscales somewhat moored has been quite an accomplishment. She has been there when I needed her most, and though our worlds are different, we have a connection that couldn't be stronger.

Late in the afternoon, I took off to Boston by myself. By now, it is obvious that while I truly enjoy people, being alone is never an issue for me. I headed to Quincy Market at Fanueil Hall. I have spent countless hours enjoying the shops and bars of what is something more touristy than I usually enjoy. When I was younger it was less so, but it's very much a guilty pleasure.

The sun was setting on a quiet Wednesday evening in the bustling district. Even though it was cool, I sat outside at a bar having a beer and watched as occasional families and couples moved by. My parent's anniversary was two days away and so I purchased an engraved pewter cup for the occasion. I couldn't stay for the celebration, but it was a nice feeling to be able to give it to them before I left.

Basically, I had a nice feeling, period. The tumult of an extraordinary year was subsiding. I had my health, good friends, the love of my wife and children, and I was musing on all that while at my childhood home, in the company of my loving parents.

As I sat there a thought jumped into my head. My father was a broadcaster, and obviously I followed in his footsteps. While I can honestly say he wasn't the inspiration for what I did, he clearly had an impact. He taught me how to breathe and speak properly. He brought me to his workplace so many times, I had no thought that there was anything special or different about what is a special and different profession. He was very good at what he did, and late into his life he brought his passion and excellence to teaching the craft at Emerson College.

He was always very proud of me, and reveled in the successes I had. Covering the World Series in consecutive years was certainly one of my greatest highlights. I had with me a tangible token of that, my World Series' media credential.

I drove back to Framingham and dug into my luggage and hauled out the elaborate credential with my picture on it hanging from a red, white and blue lanyard. My dad was lying down in his study watching TV. I asked him to stand up, I hung the lanyard over his neck and gave him a hug. It was quiet for a while, and while neither of us shed tears, it was mighty close.

He finally looked at me with moist eyes and said, "Thank you, my son."

ACKNOWLEDGEMENTS

A book like this has inspiration and perspiration from so many I hope anyone not mentioned will not be offended. First off I would like to thank my editor Mark Stallard. While I was pretty steadfast and stubborn that this would be my book, it would not have gone anywhere without his advice, toil, and sharpening. I wrote the book mainly for me, and wasn't even sure that I would try to get it published, but he and others encouraged me to take this route. He was professional and supportive, and on top of that fun to be around. It was great fun to meet his baseball playing boys, Walt and Nate, reminding me of my days in their shoes.

In no order whatsoever, I would thank many others profusely. Matt Fulks, who was the original editor, but who was honest enough to admit his plate was too full to devote proper time to my effort. Matt directed me to Mark, and it was seamless.

Kevin Kietzman, who wrote the forward, and Todd Leabo, my two compatriots on *Between the Lines*, my main forum of many at WHB. They were two of the just three people who knew I would head out on my journey. The other was my sister Colleen, who shared the secret and helped make sure the reasons were clear to my wife. Everyone in my immediate family inspires me in one way or another, and every one of them is part of the tale told here, although I generally tried to keep personal stuff about anyone but me to a minimum. My mom and dad, my three brothers and two sisters all were important influences on what I have become.

WHB is my work home and it is a great one. My thanks to

everyone from Chad Boeger at the top on down. They were all very supportive during my treatment, and create a fun environment that is reflected in some of the stories you will read. All of the on-air guys like Kurtis Seaboldt, Soren Petro, Doug Stewart, Steven St. John, Nate Bukaty, Jake Guitterez, T.J. Carpenter, Cody Tapp, and others are great to be around. I also have the pleasure of co-hosting other shows with Jack Harry and Stan Weber. There are and have been too many support people to mention here, but they are so valuable and make things click.

The old adage that you can't judge a book by its cover has never really rang true to me. If I don't like the cover of a book, I might not pick it up. Lauren Goldman did a great job designing the cover—I hope the book is as good as her work.

I would like to thank Dr. Lisa Shnayder, the incredible surgeon at KU Medical Center who did my surgery. Within months, you could barely tell that I had an incision that ran from the back of my right ear to my Adam's apple. Dr. Xinglei Shen is my radiologist and also was invaluable (and he also provided a great anecdote). All of the medical professionals at KU Med were great, and the radiation nurses come in for special note, making each day's treatment not quite so onerous.

Thanks to my daughters, Cassady and Kennedy, just for being you. Through some difficult circumstances they provided joy and sometimes heartache, but were always loved. I tried through logistical challenges to be there as much as I could, and now as young ladies, they are finding their way in the world. I love them very much, and am glad to still be around to enjoy them for a long time.

Finally, my wife Jayne. She gets many props in this book, which is dedicated to her, and she should. Most husbands wouldn't have even thought about doing what I did by just vanishing, and many told me I was insane, but I knew that she is passionate enough about me to let me be a little crazy.

Liar on the finally. I would like to thank all of the thousands of people who have listened to me through the years. You may not know it, but you are inspiring, even those who don't much like what I say. Hundreds of you emailed me when I went on the radio the day I was declared cancer free and told my story, noting the impact it had had.

I will never forget it.

ABOUT THE AUTHOR

Danny Clinkscale is an award-winning sports broadcaster who fills various hosting and reporting roles at 810 WHB in Kansas City. He is a co-host on the highly-rated *Between the Lines* afternoon drive show, hosts Baseball Tonight, College Football Gameday, co-host of Kansas City Chiefs postgame coverage, and is the station's main traveling reporter covering events such as the Super Bowl, Final Four, Baseball All-Star game, MLB playoffs, and World Series. He also has been a play-by-play announcer at the Division One level in hockey and basketball, MLS soccer, the Baseball Hall of Fame game, and many other sporting events and venues.

A graduate of the University of Kansas, Clinkscale resides in Shawnee, Kansas. The father of two beautiful daughters, Cassady and Kennedy, he is married to the lovely and talented Jayne Siemens.

Leaving Cancer for the Circus is his first book.

39284065R10122

Made in the USA
San Bernardino, CA
23 September 2016